Cambridge Elements

Elements in New Religious Movements
Series Editor
Rebecca Moore
San Diego State University
Founding Editor
†James R. Lewis
Wuhan University

EARLY TWENTIETH CENTURY NEW BLACK RELIGIOUS MOVEMENTS IN THE UNITED STATES

Darrius D. Hills
Grinnell College

Shaftesbury Road, Cambridge CB2 8EA, United Kingdom

One Liberty Plaza, 20th Floor, New York, NY 10006, USA

477 Williamstown Road, Port Melbourne, VIC 3207, Australia

314–321, 3rd Floor, Plot 3, Splendor Forum, Jasola District Centre,
New Delhi – 110025, India

103 Penang Road, #05–06/07, Visioncrest Commercial, Singapore 238467

Cambridge University Press is part of Cambridge University Press & Assessment,
a department of the University of Cambridge.

We share the University's mission to contribute to society through the pursuit of
education, learning and research at the highest international levels of excellence.

www.cambridge.org
Information on this title: www.cambridge.org/9781009534451

DOI: 10.1017/9781009534499

© Darrius D. Hills 2025

This publication is in copyright. Subject to statutory exception and to the provisions
of relevant collective licensing agreements, no reproduction of any part may take
place without the written permission of Cambridge University Press & Assessment.

When citing this work, please include a reference to the DOI 10.1017/9781009534499

First published 2025

A catalogue record for this publication is available from the British Library

A Cataloging-in-Publication data record for this Element is available from the
Library of Congress

ISBN 978-1-009-53447-5 Hardback
ISBN 978-1-009-53445-1 Paperback
ISSN 2635-232X (online)
ISSN 2635-2311 (print)

Cambridge University Press & Assessment has no responsibility for the persistence
or accuracy of URLs for external or third-party internet websites referred to in this
publication and does not guarantee that any content on such websites is, or will
remain, accurate or appropriate.

For EU product safety concerns, contact us at Calle de José Abascal, 56, 1°, 28003
Madrid, Spain, or email eugpsr@cambridge.org

Early Twentieth Century New Black Religious Movements in the United States

Elements in New Religious Movements

DOI: 10.1017/9781009534499
First published online: November 2025

Darrius D. Hills
Grinnell College
Author for correspondence: Darrius D. Hills, hillsdar@grinnell.edu

Abstract: African American religions include faith orientations that incorporate and deviate from Afro-Protestantism. Yet, contemporary scholarship in religious studies is always bolstered by any supplementary work that examines the plethora of "extrachurch" orientations that Black communities adopt in their varied pursuits of truth, transcendence, and ultimacy. In this vein, it is necessary to recognize the emergence of powerful alternative religious movements that provided spiritual and theological sustenance for the expression of Black faith. This Element offers a historical overview of four of these traditions: Conjure and Spiritualism, the Nation of Islam, the Moorish Science Temple of America, and African American varieties of New Thought. It explores the social and cultural factors in American society and American race relations that bolstered their emergence and considers the impact such movements had and continue to have on ideas about Black selfhood, Black religious authority, and the sacrality of Black bodies.

Keywords: Religio-racial identity, Black religion, American religious cultures, New Religious Movements

© Darrius D. Hills 2025

ISBNs: 9781009534475 (HB), 9781009534451 (PB), 9781009534499 (OC)
ISSNs: 2635-232X (online), 2635-2311 (print)

Contents

Introduction – Black Religion and Identity Negotiation in America   1

1 African American Conjure and Spiritualist Traditions   4

2 "Negroes" No More: Religio-Racial Reframing in the Nation of Islam   20

3 Good Moors, Good Americans: Race and Citizenry in the Moorish Science Temple of America   31

4 Holy Race(less) Angels: Father Divine and the International Peace Mission Movement   42

Conclusion – Reading Blackness Rightly: The Impact of New Religious Movements on Black Selfhood   57

References   63

Introduction – Black Religion and Identity Negotiation in America

In *Scenes of Subjection: Terror, Slavery, and Self-Making in the Nineteenth Century*, Saidiya Hartman considers how perceptions of the (in)humanity of the enslaved African functioned to create a unique subject status positionality; this required varied reproachments of power upon the captive Black body to enact spaces of agency underscoring the "metamorphosis of chattel into man [sic] and citizen" (Hartman 1997: 6). Hartman accentuates the tendency of marginalized (and minoritized) communities to look for internal recourse and resources to reframe the mode(s) of their existence, including the safeguarding of their integrity, their bodies, and their very self-conception. The tools of empowerment deployed by Black communities to contest the nature and social implications of their former enslavement, as well as the racialized regimes of Jim Crowism, were shaped by emancipatory pursuits of self-affirmation and self-definition. This Element argues that activism and identity negotiation, through the prism of alternate modes of religious faith not beholden to dominant Black church culture, provides a powerful means for the self-(re)construction and survival of Black communities in an anti-Black world.

In noting the activist and identity-based concerns that have accompanied and grounded Black religious communities' navigation of American life, I am mindful of the tendency to link such approaches with "proto-nationalist" communalism, or the setting apart of Black religious groups under the auspices of governance that is potentially theocratic in nature (Baer and Singer 2002: xvi). While this is an iteration that is key for some movements, religious nationalism is not always a uniform theo-political fixture. What I wish to emphasize here, however, is the extent to which African Americans, drawing upon their varied degrees of religious authority and agency, have carved out opportunities for religious meaning-making that centralize a unique fusion of racial *and* religious identity formation. As documented in this Element, the religio-racial movements under review allowed African American believers to reorient their racial and social standing in American society in manners that privileged racial identity during historical periods in which such self-construction was unimaginable for racialized communities.

During the early twentieth century, the ebb and flow of migration patterns that channeled African Americans into varied locales in the urban north, east coast, and midwestern cities also inaugurated new religious orientations. The engagement of this Element is not meant to be exhaustive on the rise of these religions, but rather is meant to highlight an aspect of African American religious experience as an empowering tool for identity reconstruction. To ground this Element's focus, I've opted to single out the emergence of New Black Religious Movements (NBRMs) during this historical period. The theoretical insights of religious historian Judith Weisenfeld are crucial here.

In *New World A-Coming: Black Religion and the Great Migration*, Weisenfeld develops the idea of "religio-racial" organizations to describe the coterie of the NBRMs covered in this Element. Per Weisenfeld, these religions, primarily comprised persons of African descent who "believed that understanding black people's true racial history and identity revealed their correct and divinely ordained religious orientation" (Weisenfeld 2017: 5). As a concept, "religio-racial" provides an apt descriptive iteration for these religious movements, in that it centralizes the saliency of race and/or racial philosophies as conduits of ultimate and sacred meaning. To be sure, the religious movements reviewed in this Element have varied theologies, sacred imaginaries, and divine origin stories and histories. The common factor within all, however, is the proactive and agential role of African American discernment among believers and searchers seeking new spaces and sites for religious meaning-making that also affirmed and reshifted the nature of US-based enframements of race, nation, and identity.

The African quest for meaning and personhood in North America has been impacted by a unique, if not insidious, racial legacy marked by anti-blackness. This is why the writer and essayist James Baldwin (1924–1987) once referred to identify fashioning and construction in African American life as an achievement, marked by multiple social and ideological pitfalls (Baldwin 1998: 279). Religious faith and community, in the context of religio-racial movements in the twentieth century and beyond, served the ends of this grand achievement. When, for example, new Muslim converts to the Nation of Islam rejected personal names and the racial nomenclature bequeathed by both Christian and American culture, and instead embraced Islam as the "natural religion" for the Black man and woman, they aligned their racial and religious selves in a manner more conducive to *whole* personhood. Race and religious meaning(s) were effectively fused into a symbiotic whole. Thus, NBRMs serve a pragmatic quality in that they are organizations that enabled discerning African Americans to redirect their racial, cultural, and ultimate concerns as a navigational tool for survival and spiritual sustenance in America.

Applying insights from comparative theorist and historian of religion Charles Long (1926–2020), we may say that religion is about orientation – representing the existential, cultural, linguistic, and geographical efforts of human communities to carve out a sense of place and space in their material and social life-worlds (Long 1986). During the Great Migration, Black communities in the United States faced displacement, disorientation in urban settings, and unstable economic resources. In response, religious life and religious community-making provided possibilities for personal fulfilment, softening the blows wrought by the racial, social, and economic woes that coupled the migratory shifts going on in the larger context. In adopting NBRMs, these communities eked out spaces of the familiar in a world that denied them any semblance of belonging. But more than familiarity, these new religious orientations extended the landscape of religious options that Black communities could deploy and practice, offering alternate theologies and institutional arrangements that reimagined their humanity anew in the underbelly of America's failed social experiment regarding democracy along racial lines.

Yet, this Element is not meant to be an exhaustive historical overview or a full theological appraisal of all such religious movements, but rather touches upon a few of the notable traditions that allowed Black religious communities of multiple stripes to sustain and defend Black personhood and reconfigure the nature and terms of Black identity in the early twentieth century. The central movements under review include the Nation of Islam (NOI), the Moorish Science Temple of America (MSTA), and Father Divine's Peace Mission (PM) Movement. I've chosen to proceed with this short study through six sections, including the introduction and conclusion. As a herald of African Americans' ability to embrace *alternative spiritualities and religious orientations*, the first section is not an appraisal of an NBRM proper, but rather provides an interpretation of Conjure and Spiritualist traditions. While I do not consider these practices in the same category as the religious movements under review, I felt the need to include a discussion that touched on the autonomous religious lives of the African and African American enslaved and free populations to properly accentuate the capacity of persons of African descent to effectuate religious choices beyond the limits of Protestant Christianity. This mirrors similar kinds of religious agency and authority invoked by later twentieth-century African Americans who opted for new religious movements that centered Black identity.

The second and third sections cover the NOI and the MSTA, which spotlight varied interpretations of African American Islam. These traditions are fascinating examples of the fusion of nuanced, specific understandings of blackness – Black bodies, Black histories, and Black culture(s) – with sacrality. Notably, the theologies of the NOI and MSTA are grounded in conceptualizations of Black divinity that repudiated the anti-Black animus operative in Western, Euro-American societies, past and present. I conclude with attention to African American New Thought traditions, which emphasize the power and promise of right thinking and positive mindsets as weapons to combat the ill effects of race/racism and poverty. Centered upon Father Divine's International PM Movement, I hold that this religious group did and does not explicitly hold to an emphasis on race, but on the contrary *reads through* racialized thought as illustrative of a negative, spiritually bereft psychology that harms the human condition and social relationships. For African Americans who appealed to New Thought philosophies to reconceive and reshape their material realities, the turn toward a renewed psychology on the race question proffered new sites of meaning not always captured in mainstream, liberal, and progressive Christian theological expression(s). This Element concludes with some brief reflections on the value of studying new religious movements among African American communities as a means of pursuing agency and authority in their efforts to confront the vicissitudes of race and racism.

1 African American Conjure and Spiritualist Traditions

To some degree, all the religious movements addressed in this Element are marked by a pragmatic utility that animates the motivations and rationales of its faith leaders and participants. This is perhaps more pronounced, however, for African American Conjure traditions and Spiritualism, particularly in the religious practices of enslaved and free Black populations, including and up to the nineteenth and twentieth centuries. In his efforts to map a pragmatic approach to the study of African American religion, as well as its place in the historical conditions of the Black diaspora, Eddie Glaude Jr. notes that African American religions, broadly speaking, capture the appropriate lexicon and belief structures that have allowed Black people to pursue varied mechanisms of meaning-making in an anti-Black world. He writes:

> The horrors of slavery, the terror of Jim Crow, and the myriad ways in which black people in this country have responded to the absurdity and joy of their conditions of living reveal religion as not only a crucial site for the arduous task of resisting white supremacy but also an important resource in the vexing work of self-creation under captive conditions. (Glaude 2018: 7)

One of the profound qualities of Black religions has been their unique application of the sacred imagination toward the lived experiences of the African diaspora in ways that safeguard and, in some cases, sacralize Black humanity and personhood. In part what makes Black sacred imaginative pursuits fascinating are their unique histories of spiritual and religious openness to adopting and blending seemingly polemical religious orientations, artifacts, iconography, and rituals in the formation of sacred alternatives and belief structures that buttress Black religious meaning-making. In taking Glaude's insights regarding the practical usage of religion in the Black imagination seriously, this section explores African American Conjure and Spiritualism as features of the pragmatic religiosity adopted in Black religious life and as components of the alternative religious movements that initiated new sites of meaning and ultimacy in Black notions of the sacred.

Both Conjure and Spiritualism represent distinctive religious orientations in the religious imaginations and worldviews throughout the African diasporic context. It is not my intent to suggest that either religious orientation exhausts our theoretical understanding of early African and African American religions. I highlight these belief structures mainly to illustrate the innovative and authoritative manner with which persons of African descent drew upon these traditions to create and construct meaning in their lives and to shape their lives through "extrachurch" orientations and theologies. And while these traditions are not necessarily "new" religious movements in the sense that they often derived from other streams of thought and philosophical underpinnings, what is original was their application toward the larger end of Africana religious meaning-making and the harnessing of spiritual power for the betterment of Black life. Conjuring traditions bring together varied West African ritual practices pertaining to healing, helping, or harming others. Emerging within the context of slavery in the American South, Black Conjure women and men relied upon the use of seemingly mundane, natural items and merged these with what they perceived to be supernatural power and supernatural outcomes. As such, conjurers were believed to harbor a unique spiritual expertise and knowledge about the material world and its connection to spiritual well-being and good fortune (Clark and Stoddard 2019: 17).

In the case of Spiritualism, this orientation, with roots in philosophical and religious discourses beyond the African American context, centers on the practice of traversing the material and spiritual planes of human existence and communicating with the immaterial realm – namely with the spirits of the dead. Spiritualists were gifted people who had the ability to harness their own power to contact otherworldly energies, thereby shedding light on the mysteries of nonmaterial reality and thus, shaping the meaning and hopes for present and future life. As we shall discover, African Americans who practiced Spiritualism often did so to effect particular shifts in their material existence in American society – directly confronting the social conventions and norms tied to race-based hierarchies. Before addressing these traditions and their impact on the landscape of Black religious meaning-making, it is necessary to offer historical and contextual observations on African religious experience and the impact on later creative expressions of the African American religious imagination.

Africans Were Not Religious Tabula Rasa

I concur with Peter Paris's view that African American religious experience cannot be grasped apart from the "religious and moral ethos of its African homeland" (Paris 1994: 20). This continuity is important to embrace, as it prevents myopic interpretations of the religious and cultural agency of communities across the African diaspora. It is also necessary to interpret African and African American religious context(s) in the vein of spiritual, psychic, and communal pursuits for self and collective reclamation, and the safeguarding of cultural integrity against the threat of cultural erasure. In considering the consequences and motivations that contour the American "experiment" and the place of Black people therein, Audre Lorde's declaration stated it best: Africans, and by default all Black diasporic communities that found themselves on American soil, "were never meant to survive" (Lorde 2007: 42). The life worlds and social worlds that operationalized American slavery carried an imperialist and colonialist impetus designed specifically to "otherize," or render perpetually suspect and distant, Black bodies and ways of being.

Sociologist Orlando Patterson spoke well to this distinction as *social death*, thereby elaborating upon the large-scale social ostracizing and alienation marked by both rigid hierarchies and a racial calculus tied to slavocracy. In his view, enslavement reified two vestiges of social death: *intrusive* death, which creates a permanent enemy on the inside of the dominant society, as the slave is a product of an already-alien culture, and *extrusive* death, which signifies the inevitable failure of the slave to fully integrate with the dominant group due to shortcomings in meeting legal, socioeconomic, and citizenship-based norms (Patterson 2003: 104–6). These forms of social death created a permanent underclass along with an ontologically inferior status for Blacks, which subjected the cultural and religious productions of Black communities to derision and dismissal. Regarding the role of religion and the implementation of regimes of power that bolstered the standing of the Western world at the expense of Black bodies and Black ways of being, we must also consider the effective fusion between religion and the emergence of White/European racial empire throughout Africa, the Americas, and among indigenous Americans.

As Sylvester Johnson has documented, the emergence of racial capitalism and imperialism is linked to the machinery of a religious authority, in which "the business of Atlantic empire…was concerned with racial slavery" (Johnson 2015: 117). In this dynamic, or rather, this relational power imbalance, the United States, and its attendant cultural productions, including its religious frameworks, function in tandem as a colonial enterprise, shaping the racial and religious encounters between natives, Africans, and Europeans. A consideration of the intersections of race, capitalism, colonial conquest, and empire is useful to the interpretation of Black religious experience in the New World because it prompts an acknowledgment of the centrality of colonial logics (in which Protestant Christianity and Catholicism are formidable theo-political fixtures) as a form of governance over both the racial economy and "properly" accepted/acceptable religious orientations therein. Furthermore, even race, in its initial construction(s), notes Johnson, is a "colonial governance administration through the frame of essential differences among human populations" (Johnson 2015: 88). What this means is that the racial state functions as a systemic frame for human relationships and differences – with the differences of racial and ethnic groups serving as a proxy for notions of human value. Given the centrality and pervasiveness of Western Christianity in this historical drama, it is critical to spotlight how Christendom and Euro-American colonialism shapes the religious dimensions of racialized constructions, beliefs, and practices.

It was in response to these variable and pervasive sites of dehumanization and the denial of cultural and social agency, driven by a colonialist and imperialist impetus, that the seeds of Black religious and theological imaginative capacities flowered. To be sure, African communities were already well acquainted with god/s prior to contacts with the Western world. Black theologian Dwight Hopkins' review of slave spirituals and historical documentation of religious lives among the enslaved indicates a pronounced and sophisticated religious worldview and theological imagination. According to Hopkins: "Enslaved Africans brought a distinct perception of God to North America. African traditional religions described their ultimate divinity as the High God" (Hopkins 2003: 793). Indeed, conceptions of the supreme High God in traditional African religions echo both the monotheism and classic theistic attributes typically ascribed to orthodox Christian theology.

Africans were not, therefore, tabula rasa in their religious orientation prior to enslavement. That many of the traditional African religious orientations were spliced with monotheistic theologies and notions of the sacred, likely served as a point of continuity for Africans in their introduction to Christian teachings from their enslavers. The larger issue, however, is that any recognition of Africans' pre-New World religious worldview(s) prompts an acceptance of the Africans as *religious authorities* in their own right. This view contradicts the idea that Africans (and later African Americans) were passive in their religious discernment, praxis, and beliefs. To deny the multiplicity of religious worldviews of Africans *prior* to contacts with North America and the West is to trivialize and dismiss their unique capacity to be religious authorities in their own theological imagination(s) that were contradistinctive to those rigidly associated with Jewish and Christian thinking.

Interruptions and New Creations

As historian of religions Albert Raboteau noted in *Slave Religion: The "Invisible Institution" in the Antebellum South*, the sojourn of Africans to the United States ruptured their religious frameworks (2004). Paris echoes this argument, observing that the rupture of the continuity between African communities and African traditional religions speaks to "the demise of the specific content of African cosmological thought, namely, its sacred symbols, ritual practices, particular divinities and ancestral spirits." Regardless of this interruptive break, African spirituality maintained a staying power and coherence throughout the diasporic world, often through varied expressive forms (Paris 1994: 33). The "death of the Gods" also occasioned sites of creative religious hybridization allowing for new Black religious orientations that defied racial and religious hegemonies of White society. It is the staying power of African and African American religious worldviews that most captures the interpretive interests in this chapter. What allowed these communities to "keep on keeping on" when it seemed their freedom and their gods' power were on shaky terrain for penultimate deliverance? It was between the squeeze of these quandaries that African Americans withdrew into their own primordial and material resources to revive new religious frameworks that safeguarded their new sacred identities but also served the correlated function of preserving those African-based traditions, norms, and customs that were so essential to their personhood and Blackness.

Africans brought varied traditions of religious meaning-making to the New World and fused those practices with their coerced exposure to Protestant Christianity and theology. As Hopkins notes: "Enslaved Africans took the remnants of their traditional religious structures and meshed them together with their interpretation of the biblical narrative as it was presented to them" (Hopkins 2003: 79). To be sure, however, while the White surveillance state and roving patrollers were well sourced and often made great strides in barring independent religious congregationalism among the enslaved, they adapted and found a workaround by adopting clandestine worship spaces in the "Invisible Institution." These secret, and illegal, religious worship services, "bush arbor meetings" as they were called, allowed enslaved religious cultures to feed upon a spirituality in which they communicated with God using their own cultural expressiveness and resources.

More than simply a description of the spatial and geographical description of the religious lives of the enslaved, the historical realities of clandestine religiosity among the enslaved represented the extent to which these communities and their progeny were able to live into a spiritual creativity and authoritative process of religious discernment that opened themselves and their imaginative capacities to new(er) configurations of ultimacy and sacrality – beyond the restrictive confines of White, Protestant Christianity. The relegation of Black communities to the status of the Other – both ontologically and in terms of spatial distancing in the visual and discursive regimes of Whites – occasioned sites for the creation of new horizons of meaning for African and African American life. It was therefore within moments of discursive and metaphysical discernment within community that Blacks drew upon their spiritual and religious imaginations *and* those of dominant society to create new traditions and spiritual practices that aided their ability to safeguard personhood and primordial significance against the throes of racial, political, and social disenfranchisement.

Conjure and Spiritualism as Pragmatic Religiosity

For enslaved communities, Conjure was merged with the imposed Christian worldviews bequeathed by their enslavers. Scholar of Black diasporic religions Yvonne Chireau defines Conjure as a magical tradition in which spiritual power is invoked for healing, protection, and self-defense purposes. In considering conjuring traditions, one theoretical concept is useful to keep in mind: *religious syncretism*, in which the religious orientations of Africans/African Americans were preserved and retained even as they were incorporated into Christian beliefs. While Conjure and Christianity seem to be opposites as religious orientations and in terms of theological sensibilities, Chireau spotlights the ease with which many African Americans, enslaved and free, "moved between Christianity, Conjure, and other forms of supernaturalism with little concern for their purported incompatibility" (Chireau 2006: 12).

It was not uncommon, for example, for Black clergy to adopt Conjure-based rituals to achieve certain positive outcomes. Chireau recounts an interview with an amateur folklorist in which an unnamed twentieth-century pastor was offered a "charm" from a Conjure man, which would help him bolster his fledgling church membership. The pastor finally accepted the Conjure charm "and found to his surprise the very next week that his church was full" – and remained so for four years, with crowded aisles every Sunday (Chireau 2006: 12). Chireau draws upon this historical anecdote as an example of the "persistence" of magical ideas among African American Christians, a demonstration of the extent to which charms were thought to be supplemental religious powers, and illustrative of the pragmatic utility of Spiritualist practices for African Americans. More broadly, such cases also reveal that for African American Christians who dabbled in Spiritualism, potential theological incompatibility was not so concerning that it deterred them from trying to access an alternate form of otherworldly power they were not privy to vis-a-vis the standard religiosity of Christianity or mainstream society.

It is critical to keep in mind the profound insurgent quality of conjure work and practice during slavery and in slavery's afterlives. Black Conjure practitioners often did their work as part and parcel of a subterranean religious and social network which both recognized their humanity and shielded their spiritual practices and personal integrity from the slights of a religious particularism that favored Protestant and Catholic orientations. Conjuring traditions allowed for a refusal of some of the machinations of an anti-Black world that stifled the full flowering of Black religious expression, even as, given the pervasiveness of syncretistic blending, Black religious practitioners incorporated some elements of White religious praxis. Thus, these Black Conjure practitioners, and even later Spiritualists, are appropriately deemed "underworld" religious workers, and through their varied labor(s), "they stretched beyond the enclosures of this world, into the depths of the underworld, and there they revered covert gatherings and economies, spirits and hauntings, ancestors and afterlives"

(Greene-Hayes 2025: 7). Though these worlds were imagined and deemed lesser by dominant White society, they nonetheless proved to be critical sites through which Blacks could inaugurate and maintain religious agency and innovation in their pursuits to craft new worlds and meaning that spoke to their ultimate concerns.

The religious innovation and creativity of practitioners of conjuring also extended toward the adoption of material from the natural world. "Charms," or material objects believed to be storehouses for sacred and divine entities and power, were adopted into the overall network of beliefs for religious practitioners. Charms were often mundane items, such as certain stones, small bags with natural items, or clothing deemed spiritually significant or harnessing otherworldly power. Belief in the efficacy of charms as a feature of Conjure is linked in part to the assimilation of European traditions. European Christians, particularly Catholics, placed great faith in charms, including sacramental objects, crosses, and other religious icons to bring good fortune, ward off evil spirits, and offer protection from everyday dangers (Long 2001: 11). Cultural attachment to charms among Black conjurers also has parallels to African religious practices, reflecting shifting influences over time. Chireau argues, for example, that *gris-gris* (from the Mande language) charms were ubiquitous among many African tribes and were documented as such by travelers and explorers during the sixteenth and seventeenth centuries. *Gris-gris* charms could be "worn on the body or kept conspicuously about in the open to guard against misfortune and evil" (Chireau 2006: 46). Charms, particularly for the conjurer with ties to the church, therefore offered something of material and perhaps psychological significance that the theologies, doctrines, creeds, and faith claims of the church could not. Charms proffered immediate recourse in response to the spiritual and material needs of practitioners – a specialized, alternative form of religious power deviating from established Christianity that was both efficacious in its delivery and supplementary in its collaborative ties to one's own faith orientation.

The variable applicability of Conjure traditions among enslaved African Americans suggests that strictly religious concerns were not the only motivation. On the contrary, "Conjure spoke to the practical concerns of African American bondspersons, from their personal aspirations to matters that affected everyone, such as health, wealth, and conflict" (Chireau 2006: 20). In terms of health and well-being, it is notable that conjurers were believed to render traditional medical doctors useless. If an illness or malady befell a person and traditional medical approaches offered no relief and were thought to have a malevolent spirituality as the culprit, it was the conjurer with specialization in healing practices that became the new physician. Baer classifies these Black healers, sometimes called "herbalists" and "rootworkers," as *religious specialists* who were sought after in their expertise with the specialized alchemy of plants and herbs and their use for common ailments that failed to respond to typical medical intervention, or that were the result of spiritual curses. In one Mississippi town, a "Mr. T" was renowned for his reputation as a conjurer, but self-identified as an herb doctor. Baer notes: "He does not believe in charms or voodoos, nor does he give advice in love or business affairs. He does, however, give certain medicine made from herbs, which if smeared on the body will keep away danger or attract people" (Baer 1982: 336–7, original grammar).

In African American conjuring, the spiritual causes of a disease or affliction warranted additional scrutiny.

> This does not mean that they dismissed physical or organic etiologies in their quest for explanations for the disease; it is just that their views of illness were more inclusive of external agencies. The body was the bridge that linked physical disorder and spiritual imbalance by its mediation of the two worlds. Affliction was much moreso than the physical symptoms that were so incisively described by victims as bodily states. It was viewed as a kind of attack by an invisible agent, motivated by human intent. (Chireau 2006: 100)

On some level, it may be permissible for some to be dismissive of these belief structures, particularly when considered alongside the presumed superiority of Western medicine, but it is best to err on the side of reading medicinal Conjure practices as an alternative religiosity and medical technology that enabled African Americans another avenue of wellness. There is, therefore, a performative and embodied component within the African American conjuring tradition molded specifically to the vigor, strength, and integrity of Black bodies. Theophus Smith highlights curative conjuring traditions and methods as *pharmacopeic* – bespeaking the efforts on the part of conjurers to utilize supernatural and natural resources to uplift the health of their bodies (Smith 1994: 5). In the contemporary moment, African American communities are often, structurally considered, denied access to proper medical care – and this reality was certainly more grievous in the periods during and after slavery. It therefore makes sense that Black conjurers would cultivate their own spiritual, natural, and psychic resources to address the imposed limitations. Curative conjure practices also granted its adherents a medical agency, know-how, and expertise that usurped said authority from Whites.

In this manner, for healing conjurers who appealed to their spiritual gifts as well as varied degrees of medical knowledge, their abilities as "two-headed doctors" bespeaks the insurgent quality of their religious power and authority in ways that dismantled the (White) medical establishment. As one Black woman, a trained nurse, noted, two-headed doctors "knows two kin's o' medicine…they can see both ways" (Chireau 2006: 98, original grammar). Whereas traditional medical doctors fail in their caregiving and leave patients' outcomes to the realm of chance, the Spiritualist healer "always takes Dr. Jesus [with her] and put Him in front and there is any hope He lets [her] know" (Chireau 2006: 98, original grammar). These practitioners mediate the worlds of life and death, illness and wellness. In a word, the sites and sights of the spiritual realm are not accessible by traditional routes as one seeks robust health and well-being. African American conjurers who were well versed in healing and medicinal craftwork served, therefore, as vessels through which divine power and insight could actively protect and preserve the dignities of Black lives.

Of the more salient uses of Conjure was its value in addressing racial oppression and the victimization by Whites. "Conjuring arbitrated the day-to-day conflicts in which slaves were confronted with white slaveholder domination, which was often directed and enforced through violent means" (Chireau 2006: 16). If, for example an enslaved person had the misfortune of having a brutal or sadistic overseer, conjuring "constituted a pragmatic and realistic method [of navigation and response], given a situation of extremely limited alternatives, that slaves could use to cope with their masters," and thus craft a viable means of self-defense (Chireau 2006: 17). In many such cases, which are included in the religious lore and memories of formerly enslaved communities, Black conjurers themselves were able to thwart the mistreatment of Whites in real time, thereby preserving their psychological and spiritual fortitude and reclaim some semblance of their humanity and integrity within an inhuman and demoralizing social fabric. One plantation conjurer, Dinkie, was made an example for arbitrary punishment by a zealous overseer to prove his authority. In response to the overseer's desire to "give [him] a flogging that [he would] never forget," Dinkie "gave a knowing look to the over slaves…and said, 'Ef he lays the weight ob his finger on me, you'll see de top of dat barn come off'" (Chireau 2006: 17, original grammar). That day, Dinkie avoided the lash, and further dismantled the overseer's presumed racial supremacy and authority. What happened in the barn remains a mystery, but what was apparent to the plantation congregation was the superiority of Dinkie's spiritual power, as one noted: "Dinkie's got de power...he knows things seen and unseen, an' dat's what makes him his own massa" (Chireau 2006: 17, original grammar).

In African American Spiritualism, I specifically have in mind an amalgam of supernatural practices and intellectual influences adopted by African American communities in the periods immediately following the emancipation of slavery and retained well into the twentieth century and beyond. It is useful to begin with a working understanding of Spiritualism as a religious orientation. Emily Clark and Brad Stoddard note that American Spiritualism appears to emerge during the late 1840s – containing a mix of ideas stemming from liberal religion, necromancy, seances, and spiritual mediumship. The central, grounding concept of Spiritualism centers upon belief in the capacity of flesh-and-blood human beings to traverse the immaterial planes of reality and engage otherworldly entities not seen in this life (Clark and Stoddard 2019: 39). It is worth saying a bit more about the influence of European and Catholic culture on Spiritualism and other religious and magical traditions. As was the case similarly with Conjure practices, over the periods of colonial conquest and in the midst of intermingling between enslaved Africans and the West, one net consequence of the clash of culture(s) was the assimilation of European religious frameworks, which included the practice of Spiritualism and belief in the significance and activity of the departed. As Carolyn Morrow Long observes: "European Christians believed in the reality of ghosts and spirits. The church taught that ghosts were souls caught in purgatory, unable to enter Heaven without the aid of expensive prayers and masses... Good and evil spirits – angels and demons – were thought to be in regular communication with human beings" (Long 2001: 10).

The earliest practitioners of Spiritualism were, thus, largely from White Anglo and European contexts and often their own practices and visions reinforced the racial hierarchies and stereotypes of their social worlds (see Figure 1). This observation is critical because it reveals the extent to

Figure 1 Depiction of an early twentieth-century seance among Spiritualists. Used by permission of Wikimedia Commons.

which even Spiritualist orientations were not necessarily divorced from material outcomes that implicated racial practices in the lives of fellow Spiritualists. In other words, Spiritualism, to be sure, had a particular material utility – a telos – for those who embraced it, including African Americans. The critical feature that made Spiritualism attractive was "its ability to straddle the material and spiritual worlds, the natural and the supernatural, the immediate world of those alive and the world of the dead" (Clark 2016: 7). The power and reach of Spiritualism appealed to persons of all backgrounds, as it conferred upon them the power and authority to reimagine and restructure their varied social worlds and (other) worlds.

Beyond and within the strictures of gender and race, Spiritualism enabled its followers a religious authority and agency normally reserved for established clergy in Protestant and Catholic institutions. Gender parity and the hope of egalitarian treatment represented at least one notable realm in which Spiritualism positively impacted women. As Ann Braude reveals in *Radical Spirits: Spiritualism and Women's Rights in Nineteenth Century America*, the religious authority conferred by the democratized space of Spiritualist community charted new avenues for women's religious agency at a time when such resources and opportunities were limited (Braude 2001). Yvonne Chireau's study of charismatic women's leadership in Black Spiritualist churches in early twentieth-century New Orleans likewise illustrates the pioneering legacies women Spiritualists left behind, as well as their innovate crafting of new modes of religious leadership and agency when such pursuits were imagined to be male dominated (Chireau 1998).

For the Spiritualist, attunement to matters of ultimate significance pertaining to life, death, and beyond, was a supernatural calling that was shared and open, and thus not requiring the standard catechisms or social conventions that normally validated or legitimized religious authority. The relative open-ended and democratized quality of Spiritualist orientations provided an immediate respite for Black practitioners who sought recourse from the tightly controlled auspices of conventional religious institutions. Notably, it represented a more independent religious frame for Black meaning-making and notions of the sacred. For our purposes, *Spiritualism represents beliefs that hinge upon creative religious interpretations and practices that enable one to access supernatural and sacred realms by means of their own religious authority, power, and visionary depth.* This definitional approach privileges, I believe, a proactive and pragmatic bent – notably in a way that highlights the appeal of spiritual traditions to African American communities.

The pragmatic quality of Spiritualism hearkens to the *functional* intent of African American religion that anthropologists Hans Baer and Merrill Singer cite in *African American Religion: Varieties of Protest and Accommodation*. Baer and Singer's ethnography maps a religious typology that dismantled previous monolithic interpretations of the nature of diasporic religious practices, including Islam, traditional African-derived religions, and variations of Afro-Christianity. Of note are the two guiding axes they weave into their framing of Black religious traditions: "strategies of social action" and "attitudinal orientation" (Baer and Singer 2002: 54). The former addresses how religious groups actively respond to their structural positionality in the larger society, while the latter measures the groups' level of acceptance or rejection of the values of dominant society. The strategic aspect – that is, the extent to which African American Spiritualists drew upon their visitations with the spirit world to redress and sometimes reframe components of their social and material worlds – is the primary concern. One would certainly be correct in reading "social action" as uniquely tied to, for example, the activism and protest movements associated with the Black Church and the long civil rights era.

Established and mainstream denominations in the Black community such as the African Methodist Episcopal Church, the National Baptist Convention, USA, or the Christian Methodist Episcopal Church have a long history of engagement within African American political struggles for liberation. Interestingly, many White Spiritualists tended to have progressive ideals that aligned with the grassroots activism of many Black churches. During the Civil War era, Spiritualism had robust links to radical reform movements, some of which included abolitionism, women's suffrage, and labor rights – effectively wedding religious beliefs with political causes in antebellum America (Lause 2016). African American Spiritualist practices served ends for the communities that believed in and lived by the power these practices harbored, as well as their broader material impacts. Access to the spiritual realm and to ancestral spirits guiding their paths provided otherworldly solace that intervened in the ebbs and flows of post-antebellum and Reconstruction societies. Toward this end, for both enslaved and free communities of African Americans, Spiritualism had a multitude of applications – namely safeguarding their dignity and humanity, assisting their capacities to work through grief, protecting themselves from harm and perceived danger, and establishing a basis for imagining, envisioning, and working toward the kinds of changes they hoped would upend the racial confinements of their time.

One cannot overstate the pragmatic value of Spiritualism among African American practitioners. Like conjurers, African American Spiritualists must be credited with adopting Spiritualism as a *supplementary* religious orientation that, in a penultimate sense, augmented their material realities. In other words, Spiritualism *did something*, tangibly, for African American practitioners. Emily Suzanne Clark's research on Afro-Creole Spiritualism in New Orleans at the turn of the nineteenth century spotlights some considerable findings toward this end – namely the ways in which African American Spiritualists grafted their experiences within the spiritual realm onto their aspirational hopes for new social status and a sense of place in the racial hierarchies of American society. Basing her religious history on the experiences of the *Cercle Harmonique* ("Harmonic Circle"), Clark draws upon this group's seance records and personal narratives to reveal how one consortium of Black Spiritualists leveraged their religious experiences and visions in the spiritual world toward a robust social critique of the shortcomings and failures of American democracy. The Cercle Harmonique was a collective of primarily Afro-Creole men who conducted weekly seances in which they communicated with the deceased between 1858 and 1877. The members of this cohort were all free men of color, predominantly Catholic, well educated from middle-class families, and hailed from mixed-race backgrounds including French, African, and Spanish. Clark's study relies upon the Cercle's extensive seance records and narratives, which underscored the group's overall philosophy and detailed their experiences and visions stemming from their communication with the dead.

One recounting, recorded during a seance among members of the Cercle Harmonique on September 4, 1874, the spirit of President Abraham Lincoln promised that those "who have participated in the shedding of [innocent blood]" would receive a "heart-rending" lesson in retribution (Clark and Stoddard 2019: 49). Criticizing the tyrannies of oligarchical encroachment, despotism, and greed that operationalized America's slavocracy and its judicial paradigm, the departed Lincoln's warnings of impending doom for a society rooted in inequality indicted the existing powers in post-Civil War America. These and many other messages from the spiritual realm that the Cercle accessed provided new hope and new aspirations for a livable future for America's Black community. The free exchange of racialized communities, past and present, dead and alive, is not unremarkable in this context. That free men of color harnessed their own spiritual power(s) to initiate contact with immaterial planes of existence inhabited by Whites, illustrates a religious and otherworldly sensibility in which the arbitrary markers of race held no true, lasting sway.

The Cercle, unlike other Spiritualist cohorts of the time, harnessed a brand of religious power and sacred authority that built upon their progressive demand for the creation of a new America. This collective sought power within the spiritual realm to create and inhabit "a religious world that intertwined political activism, social reform, and a moral vision for a more egalitarian United States" (Clark 2016: 4). As the Cercle was founded in the period after the Civil War and experienced its apex at the height of the Reconstruction period, it is critical to keep in mind that this historical moment was marked by precarious social and legal landscapes for African American communities. In addition to the general chaos of recalibrating community and personhood after generations of enslavement, Black communities also faced legal and extralegal threats, like disenfranchisement and violence in the forms of racial terrorism and lynching. In response to these realities, the Cercle sought recourse in the spiritual realm – finding within that space and their contacts with the spirits of the departed new religious and psychic power that centered around "the Idea."

"The Idea" repurposes the mantra for *liberté, egalité, and fraternité* (freedom, equality/egalitarianism, and brotherhood) from the French Revolution. The Cercle's unique brand of Spiritualism drew from the spiritual realm and spirit guides – a vision of the ideal American society that was shaped not by racial hierarchy or systems of dominance, but rather, a democratic America rooted in the promise of racial and cultural harmony. The spirits believed to guide the Cercle included former US presidents, Enlightenment thinkers, international dignitaries, local politicians, and departed family members and friends. It was from the spiritual realm's grand "Idea" that the Cercle crafted a religious and spiritual network through which they reenvisioned the human ties and belonging that should characterize, broadly, America's full flourishing as a multiracial constitutional republic. In their efforts to transplant the otherworldly racial and fraternal utopia of their spirit contacts and corresponding visions into their social setting, the Cercle furthermore distinguished itself in its belief that the spirit world was raceless, a mindset that would not have been widely shared among other White Spiritualists of the time.[1]

As it relates to the seance records, what is noteworthy of the Cercle's spiritual encounters are both the personality of the spirit contacts, as well

---

[1] *Religion Dispatches* Interview, Paul Harvey, September 20, 2016, https://religiondispatches.org/black-spirits-matter-a-spiritual-history-of-new-orleans-that-recognizes-afro-creoles/.

as the visionary quality of the spiritual world that they sought to instill into American society. After offering thanks to the "infinitely Good Father for their place on earth," the brotherhood asked "the spirits of Peace and Light to guide them, put them on the path of eternal progression, and drive away the darkness" (Clark 2016: 34). The spiritual messages that Cercle mediums received, which were recorded and transcribed in their native French, were varied and touched upon a host of religious, political, and familial concerns. Departed family members would bring messages of encouragement, as "the burden of mourning could be borne more easily by communicating with the dead and receiving assurance from loved ones that they were happy in the spiritual world" (Clark 2016: 39–40). Historical figures, such as President Abraham Lincoln's assassin John Wilkes Booth and Confederate general, Robert E. Lee appeared to apologize for past sins related to racial violence and unjust political positions.

What the Cercle drew from the spirits often shed light on the discrepancy between the idealized world of the spiritual realm, animated by equality and brotherhood, in contrast to America's racism, disharmony, and decadent pursuits of material greed. The chief, animating attributes of the spirit world provided the ground for the Cercle's "Idea" centered on the truth that "the spirit world was a far superior place in comparison to earth [because] the spirits submitted to the laws of harmony and love" and carried these ideas within their highest consciousness. Cercle members were, therefore, expected to embrace these higher expressions of enlightenment. As the spirit of Saint Vincent de Paul was believed to say to the group: "Dear children of progress: always be vigilant about the state of your heart, [for] you have to work to purify [your heart] day after day, to be worthy of the One who created you" (Clark 2016: 43). Such admonitions revealed to the Cercle that they were called to promote these spiritual and moral values toward a new vision that would allow humanity to progress into a spiritual republic unencumbered by the disharmony and estrangement that was borne of racism and failed American democracy.

Conclusion

Both Conjure and Spiritualist practices offered new religious worldviews through which African American communities reoriented values, aspired to transformative possibilities in *this world*, and imagined new futures. It is key to note how both traditions were coupled with material outcomes for the communities who adopted them. In the case of the conjurers, their manipulation of sources in the natural world, which was underscored by an abiding belief in these sources' supernatural power, enabled them to shape their destinies and fortune, even as they made use of the same to inflict harm in the name of self-defense and justice against the backdrop of the oppressive realities of Jim Crow America.

For African American Spiritualists, the visions and encounters proffered by nonmaterial planes of existence resulted in the psychic consequence of broadening their conceptualization, experience, and access to the realms of life and death – issuing forth an otherworldly impetus to incorporate these experiences in their drafting of new possibilities in America broadly, and for African Americans specifically. In the larger scheme, these religious traditions are useful case studies into the deeply utilitarian and material bent to African American religious experience and praxis – both disclosing the collective desire for new religious orientations beyond mainstream American Christendom, and also setting the stage for a cultural openness to novel ideologies, religious or otherwise, that offered discursive, practical, and ontological tools through which Black humanity could be conceived, acknowledged, and sacralized.

2 "Negroes" No More: Religio-Racial Reframing in the Nation of Islam

> It is the knowledge of self that the so-called Negroes lack which keeps them from enjoying freedom, justice, and equality. This belongs to them divinely as much as it does other nations of the earth. It is Allah's (God's) will and purpose that we shall know ourselves. Therefore He came Himself to teach us the knowledge of self. Who is better knowing of who we are than God, Himself? He has declared that we are descendants of the Asian Black Nation and the tribe of Shabazz. (Muhammad 2012)

Many a Black writer has asserted that reserving for oneself the agency to name and claim one's distinctive identity is a significant feature of personal, insurgent agency. For those of African descent, such agency takes on unique ontological meaning, revealing the proactive desire for self-assertion and self-fashioning. The African diaspora is also unique in that individuals' identities, stemming from the realities of American slavery, were largely relegated to, and defined by racialized enfleshment, or the Black body as *only body*. Sedimented in White society's racial imagination and hierarchy and further codified into law in the governance of the United States, the non-personhood and denial of the humanity of Black people was most powerfully articulated in chattel slavery and manifest in the racial apartheid of Jim and Jane Crow. What resulted from the restrictive enframement of Black personhood and humanity, was rote dehumanization.

Radical Black nationalist Eldridge Cleaver (1935–1988) once offered a philosophical breakdown of this phenomenon in his controversial 1968 book, *Soul on Ice*. Cleaver argued that the bodies of Black people were relegated to "supermasculine menial" status, while their White counterparts were tagged "omnipotent administrators" (Cleaver 1968). Yet, it is useful to furthermore make necessary connections between the religious views and theological paradigms of the Nation of Islam (NOI), and notions of Black embodiment and Black humanity. Stephen Finley observes that the American social order effectively rendered Black bodies as bodies "in place," that is, subject to whims and frameworks that sanctioned Black embodiment in manners that were "innocuous and acceptable to white communities" (Finley 2022: 5). The reification of Black people and Black bodies to static dispositions in this way provided an opportunity for the NOI to inspire African American coverts to use their religious faith and the religious meaning ascribed to Black racial heritage as an effective tool to navigate racist society.

When Elijah Muhammad (1897–1975) took up the leadership and theological mantle of NOI teachings, he brought a message to the "so-called Negro" in America. This message would help the lost and misguided Asiatic Black man and woman recover their righteous mind by living into their natural divinities as Allah's original people. A prominent feature in the process of self-recovery for NOI members was their embrace of a religious worldview that designated the divine quality of the Black body. The appropriate focus of this section addresses the uniqueness of NOI's theology of race and what kind of impact this had on the racial and religious consciousness of African American followers. NOI teachings allowed Black Muslims to reimagine and repurpose Black identity – aligning both their souls and their very Black bodies with the divine, challenging the racial calculus that rendered them inferior. The shifting and reframing of Black identity, to be sure, was ideologically linked to the religious work and ministries of other contemporaries of Muhammad, including, for example, Noble Drew Ali, who also taught a variation of Black Islamic religion – largely associated with the MSTA (see next section).

The teachings central to the founding of the NOI took root in the early twentieth-century American migration period with the emergence of a mysterious figure of dubious ethnic/national background, Wallace Fard Muhammad (1893–1934) in Detroit, July 4, 1930. On first appearance, Fard Muhammad was unremarkable as part of a subculture of eastern-based immigrants who sold food, clothing, and other goods of middle eastern fare that were advertised as from the Holy Land. But in daily visits among his urban, African American clientele, he brought much more. He preached a new religion that reoriented Black people's self-knowledge and religious devotion. The religion of Islam, Fard Muhammad claimed, was the "natural" religion for Black people, and the Christian tradition that Blacks were coerced into vis-à-vis the processes of American slavery was fraudulent and its theology denied, rather than affirmed, their divine identities as God's chosen people. In noting the early theological and racial interventions that Fard Muhammad made into his variation of African American Islam, it is critical to hold this history in tension with the broader, traditional landscape of Islamic religion, which was not formulated as a religio-racial orientation. In other words, our review of the NOI requires a healthy distinction regarding Islam as a universalized faith tradition against the particularistic Islam proffered by Fard Muhammad and later matured under the leadership of Elijah Muhammad, Malcolm X, Warith Deen Muhammad, and Louis Farrakhan (see Figure 2).

Edward E. Curtis notes that presuming a default tension in the landscape of African American Islam – namely that there is a strict binary between Islamic universalism and African American particularism – is too simplistic an interpretation. Etymologically, there is evidence that supports claims regarding the universalism of Islam; for "Islam" is literally defined as "submission" (to the will of Allah), and upholds the shared humanity of all persons, regardless of race or sex. The apt crux of the question highlighting the tension, Curtis notes, lies in "how much difference of any sort can be incorporated or tolerated within a tradition that is seen as universally applicable to all human beings, regardless of race, nation, ethnicity, or any other identifier" (Curtis 2002: 12–13). The distinctions on the nature and terms of universality versus particularity in African American Islam are helpful in dismantling essentialist claims about Islam

Figure 2 Malcolm X delivering a speech to Nation of Islam members. Used by permission of Wikimedia Commons.

and about the capacity of African American converts to mold their own unique brand of Islamic faith within their specific contexts.

Like all Black religious orientations, branches of African American Islam, including the NOI, must be contextualized against racist and racializing histories woven into the African diasporic context. It was within these contexts that Black religious persons drew upon their faith, in sometimes radical, insurgent manners, to affirm their humanity and personhood. For many Black converts, embracing the universality endemic to Islam provided hope and instilled an integrity and dignity in a way that (American) Christianity did not. It is completely necessary, therefore, to think of Black Muslims as full agents in their own religious authority and meaning-making within the context of NOI teachings, theologies, and community. In drawing on Curtis's labeling of African American Islam, and the teachings of the NOI specifically, as racially particularistic in contrast to Islamic universalism, my objective is to center "the theoretical ambiguity necessary in describing the diverse and ultimately disputed meanings of blackness espoused" among NOI members (Curtis 2002: 14).

In other words, the actual beliefs and practices of NOI adherents should be seen as demarcating a particular religious and racial community – one set apart and distinctive from the mainstream and directed toward a specific telos for Black Muslims. In noting the strong particularism in the NOI's self-assessment and understanding collectively, marking one's group as unique with its own sacred alterity would appear to be an agential and proactive safeguarding of religious identity and authority. Yet, adopting a particularist read of the NOI's theology of race also provides insight into how these communities understood the matrix of race, ancestry, nationality, and history within the contours of their religious imagination – demonstrating the unique "relationships between historical actors and the larger contexts in which they wrote and spoke" (Curtis 2002: 15). While there have been both universalistic and particularistic impulses in the landscape of African American Islam, in the case of the NOI, the particularistic bent to its theology of race proved central to Black Muslims' sacred imagination, pursuit of social liberation, and material flourishing against the backdrop of anti-Black racism.

Yakubian Lore and Liberation: The NOI's Theology of Race

Born Elijah Poole in 1897 in Sandersville, Georgia, Elijah Muhammad was an early convert to the NOI – inspired by Fard Muhammad's teachings in Detroit during the 1930s and eventually becoming its leader and chief theologian after the mysterious disappearance of Master Fard Muhammad sometime in 1934. Elijah Muhammad was noteworthy as the central proselytizer and leader of the NOI from the late 1930s until his death in 1975, and is credited, alongside Malcolm X (1925–1965), with making the NOI a prominent symbol of the Black Islamic presence in America as well as a fixture in the larger Black popular cultural imagination. Unlike other contemporaries of African American Islam, Elijah Muhammad developed a polemical religious and racial orientation for Black Muslims – which, as noted, should be considered alongside a desire for religious identity formation that addressed African Americans' salvific and material concerns. Elijah Muhammad preached an absolutist Islamic particularism that singled out the divinity and divine favor of Black bodies. Moreover, not only were Black people God's chosen covenant community; it was the White European who was racially and spiritually inferior. It was this juxtaposition – White inferiority and Black divinity – that Muhammad cast as (1) an explanation for the state of American race relations, (2) the basis for ontological reasoning regarding social, psychological, and moral disconnects among Whites and Blacks, and (3) a rationale for his doctrine of racial separatism. We may trace these topics, in part, to the NOI's teachings regarding the myth of Yakub.

The creation mythology and racial cosmology surrounding the "god scientist," Yakub, represented a core teaching of the NOI's theology of race and racial identity – one that legitimized Black Muslims' claims of divine identity and divine authority and therefore delegitimized the racist perceptions of Black (in)humanity. Over 6,000 years ago, Yakub was a member of the tribe of Shabazz, from whom modern day African Americans descended. Prior to Yakub's birth, according to this myth, Black people governed and ruled harmoniously. Yet Yakub, who was well known from his youth as being given to arrogance and prone to dissent and disharmony, sought to foment disarray, corruption, and strife. Master Fard Muhammad and Elijah Muhammad taught that Yakub's intellect and passion for disharmony culminated in what basically amounted to eugenicism – a desire to create a new race of people who were descended from the original Black race. This new race of people, who became the White, European human, was artificially created through a "germ" grafting process, in which the stronger "black" germ (gene) was spliced and manipulated (through intermarriage) with the lighter brown gene, resulting in a new genetic sequence carried forth by fully phenotypically White human beings. Whites would then rule over the original Black people for 6,000 years until the restoration of the original nation by Allah – in which the "warring, wicked world of Yakub (the Caucasian world)" – would be destroyed and the new world of liberty, righteousness, and peace would emerge (Muhammad 2012). Over time, Yakub's teachings, theology, and scientific work continued to promote disharmony throughout his community, and this led to his being exiled: "Yakub rebelled against Allah and the righteous people and was cast out of the homes of the righteous into the worst part of the planet to live their way of life until the fixed day of their doom" (Muhammad 2012).

The Yakubian theology of the NOI reveals profound implications for the assertion and reclamation of Black humanity and personhood central to NOI teachings. Primarily we may first trace the notion of divine Blackness to the cosmological assertion that Black people are God's original creation – for as the original human, Black people have no beginning and no end; Blackness is deified, for Allah [himself] is a Black man.[2] In Leonard McKinnis's ethnographic study of the theology and social practices of the Black Coptic Church community in Chicago, he notes that the Copts proffered a "theology and way of life that united [its members] to a view of Blackness that contradicted remnants of social, political, and religious orders that were tethered to anti-Blackness" (McKinnis 2023: 10). In like manner, the divinity of Blackness that the Yakubian myth safeguarded, was entrenched in the idea that Blackness and Black bodies could be and were redeemed, valued, and restored over against the machinations of anti-Black White supremacy. As Elijah Muhammad once wrote, quoting the teachings from Fard Muhammad: "above all, [Fard] says, the black man is the father, the first, and the last of all mankind. There is no GOD but him, on earth and in the space above. He proves this by the works of the black man's wisdom" (Weisenfeld 2017: 67). From a psychic standpoint, to be sure, such a theology contradicted the ideological underpinnings hinging upon the lesser humanity and inferiority of African/African Americans – thereby restoring the self-esteem and self-worth attached to being Black despite American society's determination to practice otherwise.

This myth was also critical in its promotion of Black people's moral, spiritual, and cultural superiority in contrast to White civilization, which was no civilization at all. Yakub, as Muhammad taught, given his own disposition for mischief, deception, and treachery, passed on these traits, known as the art of "tricknology," to the weaker White race, who, through its own genetic frailty, was prone to feebler moral and ethical suasions.

---

[2] In virtually all existing literature available from the NOI, God is described in masculine terms.

The spiritual and genetic flaws of the White European race were manifest in their inclination toward disagreement, moral treachery, and conflict, serving the larger end of the righteous Blacks' eventual enslavement and their psychological and social estrangement. Muhammad comments on this nefarious moral framework as follows:

> Mr. Yakub taught his made devils on Pelan: That – when you go back to the holy black nation, rent a room in their homes. Teach your wives to go out the next morning around the neighbors of the people and tell that you heard her talking about them last night. When you have gotten them [Blacks] fighting and killing each other, then ask them to let you help settle their disputes and restore peace among them. If they agree, then you will be able to rule them both. This method the white race practices on the black nation, the world over. They upset their peace by putting one against the other and then rule them after dividing them. (Muhammad 2012)

The mythological teachings on the moral differences along Black and White lines also confronted the standing racial bona fides of the past and present, which largely posits as a natural given the moral, social, and physical inferiority of Blacks. The Yakubian myth, therefore, offered a profound confrontation with the prevailing assumptions of White supremacy and had the additional effect of uplifting Black self-image and the affirmation of the physical Black body. Consider for example Muhammad's commentary on the quality of racial aesthetics for the lesser White race: "Yakub made devils who were really pale white, with really blue eyes; which we think are the ugliest of colors for a human eye" (Muhammad 2012). In a societal context that largely dismantles notions of Black aesthetic beauty, integrity, and strength, a racial theology that privileged Black superiority over against White inferiority, was potentially a psychic boon for Black self-esteem, and harbored great appeal for beleaguered African Americans who converted to the NOI. The colorism that animates this feature of the Yacubian myth hearkens to the influential "doll tests" conducted by psychologists Kenneth and Mamie Clark during the 1930s and 1940s. During these tests, when Black children were offered one of two dolls, the Black children invariably chose white dolls rather than black dolls and later iterations of the experiment revealed that children also associated negative characteristics and moral deficiencies with the black dolls and positive affirmations toward the white dolls – revealing the extent to which the racial hierarchy and social habitus in American societies cultivates self-hatred in the early psychological development among Blacks.

The myth of Yakub and the NOI's theology of race were not widely accepted in the larger landscape of traditional Islamic teaching, and as such, Sunni and Shi'a Muslim branches in America and abroad did not recognize these teachings as legitimate. Malcolm X's break from the Nation in 1964, following his public disagreements over the moral failings of Elijah Muhammad (coupled with his own doubts about the religious and theological legitimacy of the NOI), opened the door to traditional Islam. Later on, under the leadership of Elijah Muhammad's son, Warith Deen Muhammed (1933–2008), the NOI began to realign itself with the universal Islamic community of faith as a Sunni Islam organization, which he founded in 1976 a year after his father's death. In doing so, Deen Muhammed rejected the previous teachings on race in the NOI and embraced the universal brotherhood and sisterhood of all Muslims without regard for race and ethnicity. Prior to these shifts, however, for the earliest converts to the NOI, the theology of race and the racial cosmology proffered through the myth of Yakub gave these adherents a new language and origin story to embrace Black personhood in an insurgent manner that ran counter to the larger racial and cultural scripts that dominated their sojourn in American society.

Black Bodies as Black Temples: Ritual Considerations

Enjoining the theological paradigm that helped Black Muslims shift the meaning and scope of Black personhood was attention to the centrality of Black bodies – notably in terms of dietary, attire-based, and naming practices. Some of the features of the NOI's objectives in reaching, teaching, and reforming the so-called Negro in America was centered upon the struggle to find true knowledge of self. Floundering in White American society damaged Black self-knowledge and personhood by divorcing them from Islam and from the essential features of their Asiatic Muslim identities. Recovering these fixtures served two purposes. Primarily, they realigned and restored a connection to the cultural vitality of the Black/Asiatic self, homeland, and its origins. But these practices, including dietary, personal attire, and self-definition and adornment, also served a spiritual purpose that enabled Black Muslims in America to build communal pride and develop spiritual purity – thereby eschewing what they perceived to be the decadence, rot, and impropriety of (White) American culture. I highlight first the dietary laws, which Elijah Muhammad articulated in his *How To Eat To Live*.

The loss of self-knowledge was levied first upon enslaved Africans, who were coerced into foreign epistemologies and cultural practices that were not in keeping with their unique and indigenous life-worlds and communities of origin prior to contacts with the West. This much is hinted at throughout *How To Eat To Live*, as Muhammad regularly inveighs against the dietary practices of the "commercializing White race," who is not eating for health and longevity, but is only "after the almighty dollar" in the promotion of cheap, ultra-processed food (Muhammad 2018). Internal purity and cleanliness translated to spiritual purity and divine favor. Dietary restrictions were central to how Muslims understood themselves as a religious community and how they worked to discipline themselves according to Allah's will. The primary directives for dietary practice focused on two commitments: "cleanliness and health achieved through the elimination of the wrong foods, and the purity and longevity achieved through food restriction." Poisonous foods, damaging both soul and body, included pork, catfish, white breads and heavy starches, and several classes of vegetables thought to be unsuited for proper human digestion.

Muhammad also taught that fried foods and other fattening batter additions were to be discarded in favor of baked options, and meat, except for certain fish, was to be eaten in moderation if not rejected. Weisenfeld highlights Muhammad's particular targeting of Black southern cuisines as poisonous, potentially citing a larger psychospiritual motivation in which he sought to disabuse Muslims from embracing culinary cultures that were prominently tied to African American slavery – thereby calling for an excision of those practices linked to the past instead of looking forward to a new future under the divine guidance of Allah. Prompting NOI members to shift from former culinary practices associated with slavery provided Elijah Muhammad a basis to push them to "reject the familiar foods of their families and communities," and make marked distinctions between "the ways of the ignorant mired in mental slavery and those who had embraced their true religio-racial identities" (Weisenfeld 2017: 144).

The NOI also prohibited the use of stimulants and all drugs, including tobacco and alcohol, which would weaken the body, reduce moral strength, and contribute to unnecessary costs related to doctor visits and sicknesses. In addition to food restrictions and choices, also critical was how and when NOI members should eat – which prioritized the emphasis on fasting, as Muhammad writes: "Eat a single meal a day, no matter what anyone says. If your doctor says that you should eat more than one meal a day, ignore him with a smile…The more idle our stomachs are, the longer they will last. The more we tax our stomach, the sooner it wears out" (Muhammad 2018). The beliefs about fasting sync with the fasting practices observed during the Muslim month of Ramadan, thereby providing a significant religio-cultural link between the NOI and the orthodox Islamic community. On the question of alcohol and drugs, Black Muslims' abstinence from these indulgences furthermore contributed to their moral sensibilities. A clean diet promoted a clean soul, providing spiritual and psychic sustenance that fostered an avenue toward more robust communal and embodied affirmation – effectively displacing and/or challenging the accepted cultural registers built upon anti-Black nonbeing, inferiority, and moral deficiency.

Similar implications are drawn from the conservative dress and attire for NOI women and men. It was no accident, for example, that in public venues, Black Muslims were often adorned in their "Sunday best" – dark colored suits and ties for men, and modest dresses and head coverings (hijab) for women. Self-presentation of this caliber offered another means of contradicting the negative narratives about Blackness – allowing for the pursuit of an alternative Black humanity not tied to the White, American gaze. Monica L. Miller's study of "dandyism" in African American communities spotlights the roles that fine clothing and novel adornment strategies played in Black cultural sensibilities and identity formations across the Black Atlantic world. Black "styling and profiling," says Miller, allow the transformation "from costumed object designed to trumpet the wealth, status, and power of white masters to self-styling subjects who use immaculate clothing, arch wit, and pointed gesture to announce their often-controversial presence" (Miller 2009: 1). Clothing can be an insurgent countercultural tool signifying something about the individual and the larger community – as it sends messages about how each see themselves and how they want to be seen. In the case of Black Muslims, presenting their divinely sanctioned bodies to American society in their best attire safeguarded a sense of purpose and worthiness not just in the eyes of Allah but also as a defense of their humanity against the backdrop of anti-Black racism and racial apartheid.

Finally, safeguarding Black humanity was also tied to ritual naming practices that were meant to signify both a return to authentic self-knowledge and highlight the transition from mental and cultural slavery toward restored cultural and familial identity. On this score, the adopting of new names, a feature of both NOI and Moorish Science Temple members' practices, allowed these groups not only to inaugurate their own sacred narratives of rebirth highlighting new personhood but also to denounce the restrictive enframements of American cultural norms. For NOI members, adopting new names was tantamount to embracing an authentic birthright – demarcating their proactive transition from mental and psychic enslavement toward spiritual renewal more aligned with their ancestral origins.

In 1964, after completing the Hajj, or the required spiritual pilgrimage to the holy land of Mecca for all able Muslims, Malcolm X (formerly Malcolm Little) adopted the name el-Hajj Malik el-Shabazz. Of the experience of the Hajj, he wrote "My pilgrimage broadened my scope. It blessed me with a new insight" (Malcolm X 1992: 394). This new insight was grounded in a new racial and religious awakening, given Malcolm's experiences in Mecca worshipping and fasting with Muslims of different racial and class backgrounds, including Whites, in true unity and brotherhood. This awakening also inspired a change in his identity as a Black Muslim, prompting the desire for a renewed selfhood detached from the cultural mores of White American society responsible for his former last name, "Little," which he rejected. As part and parcel of the slave name and slave culture from which his African American lineage descended, Malcolm X's pilgrimage signaled an ongoing rupturing from American slavery and the start of a new identity rooted in the specificity of his religious faith as a Black Muslim.

Conclusion

The particularist iteration of African American Islam espoused by the NOI's leadership has undergone several shifts and potential mini schisms over time. Under the guidance of Elijah Muhammad's son, Warith Deen Muhammad, the NOI made attempts to shed some of its racial theology and aligned itself with the broader Islamic faith community as Sunni Muslims. With the rise of Louis Farrakhan (b. 1933), who is the present leader, however, the NOI has retained and revived some of its racial theology and has moved more stridently into Black nationalist economic leanings. While Farrakhan's tenure has been marked by some controversy, notably his beliefs about the necessity of racial separatism (a carryover from the early teachings of Elijah Muhammad), antisemitic beliefs, as well as ongoing skepticism that he remains committed to anti-White racism, there are many aspects of his religious work that reveal a progressive mindset looking to the future. Farrakhan in one respect has worked to restore the prophetic status of Elijah Muhammad as the messenger of the NOI movement as well as the traditionalism of the founder Wallace Fard Muhammad. However, Farrakhan is also notable for touting the NOI's particularism for African American Muslims while promoting an ecumenical bent in his participation in interracial and interfaith cooperation throughout the

1980s and 1990s (Curtis 2002: 131). This iteration of NOI's presence and standing in contemporary settings in part reflects our society's general acceptance of a global and pluralistic mindset among American citizens – indicating that the strict separatism of any racial or religious community is unlikely to elicit the interests of many converts, as was the case in prior generations.

Whether or not Farrakhan and the larger infrastructure of NOI believers will again adapt and shift according to the trends of our time is unknown, but what is likely to remain in place is the desire on the part of African Americans, including Black Muslims, to realize and live into a racial peoplehood that is unfiltered and uncorrupted by the racialized gaze of White supremacist culture. The racial peoplehood espoused within the NOI's teachings, and early theological worldview(s), offered another path forward beyond the White-adjacent notions of Blackness encapsulated in the description "Negro." Black Muslims were able to craft a religious and racial identity with its own sacred history set apart from the mundaneness of their American experience. For this about-face in Black religious experience, the NOI deserves immense credit for its pursuit of alternative conceptions of Black meaning-making that both critiqued and moved beyond White American religious and cultural norms.

3 Good Moors, Good Americans: Race and Citizenry in the Moorish Science Temple of America

> It is a peculiar sensation, this double-consciousness, this sense of always looking at one's self through the eyes of others, of measuring one's soul by the tape of a world that looks on in amused contempt and pity. One ever feels his two-ness, – an American, a Negro; two souls, two thoughts, two unreconciled strivings; two warring ideals in one dark body, whose dogged strength alone keeps it from being torn asunder.
>
> W. E. B. Du Bois, *The Souls of Black Folk* (2019)

The epigraph from W. E. B Du Bois offers an appropriate introduction to the ruptured self-understanding that characterizes Black experiences in (White) American society. Du Bois was trying to articulate the feelings – really, the psychology – of Black Americans struggling to reconcile themselves to life in a social habitus that was foreign, collectively precarious, and in many ways, was and remains, viciously unwelcoming. There is an added psychological layer to what Du Bois describes – notably the tensions related to Black self-image and how this is spliced and distorted by the racialized machinations endemic to America's racial economy. Part of the raced and social "two-ness" Du Bois describes involves the looming ontic caricatures of Black humanity that are driven by the combined racial gaze(s) of White society in America, rather than by the agency of Blacks' desires for self and communal ownership. Duboisian double-consciousness therefore properly frames both racial and cultural ostracization born of Black personhood within, and against, the backdrop of American life. In another regard – one befitting the purposes of this present section – the double-consciousness experienced by racially and culturally minoritized groups bespeaks the consequences of living into one's fullness "in spite of." That is to say, against the many cultural and social pitfalls that dictate the shape of Black life.

Reconciling the competing forces that provide succor and stability to Black life and personhood alongside the prevailing, dominant racial and cultural landscapes in America has left African American communities with precious few options for realizing their own unique forms of congruence and self-reclamation, and religious faith has been a keen cultural tool in this process. Our previous examination of the NOI, for example, provided an example of a Black religious orientation that crafted a theology of race and place that redefined the terms of longstanding components of American racial hierarchies by marking Black bodies and Black histories and Black futures as extensions of divine import. Moreover, the NOI also embraced a psychospiritual praxis of *Black* self-reclamation and identity formation by calling into question the legitimacy of America as central to Black self-worth and self-knowledge.

These fundamental shifts woven into NOI theologies, notably in its doctrines of racial separatism, rejected outright the need for alliances and recognition tied to the United States and its governmental apparatus. In shifting our focus to Noble Drew Ali and the teachings encapsulated by the Moorish Science Temple of America (MSTA), we encounter another fixture in the landscape of African American Islamic traditions, which also represents a historical contemporary and ideological bedfellow with the NOI. Like the NOI, the Aliites/Moors, as they were called, were unique in that they embraced the civil religiosity tied to American exceptionalism, even as they navigated and negotiated the racial and legal categorizations endemic to America's social fabric. MSTA teachings about race, citizenship, and contrasting notions of American law versus Divine Law will serve as points of reflection in this section.[3]

---

[3] Spencer Dew's *The Aliites: Race and Law in the Religions of Noble Drew Ali* provides several useful organizational distinctions that I have adopted in this section. Namely, while Ali is recognized as the leader and chief theological expositor of Moorish American

Aliite Theology and Race

Like many charismatic religious icons, Noble Drew Ali (1886–1929) – born Timothy Drew (aka Thomas Drew) and known by followers as Prophet Ali – has a mysterious history and background. But what is known and attested to by his followers was his indelible contribution to the religious and citizen-based identities of African Americans in search of place and belonging in the racial and political wilderness of North America. With birth and family roots in Virginia and North Carolina according to official and unofficial documents, Drew's lineage includes part of the great sojourn of African Americans seeking greater economic and social recompense in the Great Migration, journeying from the south toward the northeast coast, eventually settling in Newark, New Jersey. In Newark's Seventh Ward, the adult Drew found an environment awash with a wide base of international immigrant communities, including Greeks, Russians, Italians, and Irish – alongside Black migrants like himself (Weisenfeld 2017: 47). It is interesting, given this diverse localized context, to therefore consider this realm as key in the development of Drew's democratic sensibilities as well as instrumental in the flowering of his religious imagination.

Having exposure to and living and working alongside various other ethnic communities during this period may have propelled the young Drew and later the Prophet Noble Drew Ali, toward a nuanced understanding of place, space, and community uncommon among his other African American counterparts. That is, perhaps in the sea of racial, cultural, and geographic difference that characterizes urban cities in flux with booming immigrant populations, Ali was able to cultivate what Spencer Dew refers to as a philosophy of "universalized difference" – a cultural/ideological broadness that encapsulates one's understanding of their larger social world by holding their lifeworld and social context in tension with those of "others." In doing so, Noble Drew Ali was able to reaffirm the uniqueness of his own (Black) identity and history. In making this observation, it is critical to keep in mind the social, economic, and political precariousness shaping Black life in America during the early twentieth century. Like his contemporaries in the NOI, Ali sought recourse through another religious and cultural revitalization project that allowed him and his followers to reclaim their destinies and identities over against the impositions of (White) American society.

---

religious beliefs and theological orientations, there are several additional branches of the belief system that Dew addresses. I refer readers to Dew's volume for further information, since this Element limits the discussion of MSTA to the broader theological, racial, and judicial underpinnings of the group's theology and understanding of citizenship.

In the spring of 1927, Black Chicagoans had the opportunity to hear from Prophet Ali directly, who was in the early stages of establishing the Chicago MSTA temple after growing his ministry in the Newark area since 1913; it was originally known as "The Canaanite Temple" (Clark 2013: 33). One of the flyers advertising his mission to potential converts exclaimed, "Don't Miss the Great Moorish Drama," and thereby exhorted listeners and worshippers "to uplift fallen humanity and teach those things necessary to make men and women become better citizens" (Weisenfeld 2017: 43). The drama to which attendees and followers would become privy, involved the embrace of a theology and social identity that coalesced around Ali's insistence that persons of African descent in the United States were not, in fact, Negroes, but were Moorish American Muslims. Any other identity marker or title beyond this, as we shall see, was rejected as a fraudulent deviation from Black Americans' true selfhood.

Central to Ali's theology and doctrine of race was that the so-called Negroes in North America were literal descendants of present-day Moroccans, despite their physical locale and birth in the United States. The story of the American Negro's identity, in Ali's thought, was premised upon a false nationality and false religious consciousness. Moorish Americans, he declared: "had been 'marked' by Europeans with the false names of 'Negro, Black, Colored, and Ethiopia [sic]' and that these 'nicknames' kept the truth of their identity hidden" (Weisenfeld 2017: 43). Similarities shared with the NOI are apparent. Ali taught that African Americans were denied communal and self-agency, driven in part by an identity subterfuge that was endemic to the racial hierarchy of American culture. The hegemonic constructs of race and culture that blinded the Moorish people drove a wedge between African Americans' forebears and contemporary African American communities *and* ruptured the embrace of their true religious ancestry, which was best articulated through Islam. In contrast to Christianity, which Ali claimed was not a true expression of Moorish faith, Islam was held to be the first divine religious creed, and an essential feature of the nature of all descendants from Africa. Drawing upon the *Holy Koran of the Moorish Science Temple of America*, also known as the *Circle 7 Koran* (comprised of his own writings, as well as two other texts),[4] Ali declares: "There is no one who is able to change man from the descendant nature of his forefathers unless his power extends beyond the great universal Creator Allah Himself" (Weisenfeld 2017: 43).

---

[4] These additional texts, rooted in mysticism and esoteric philosophical teachings, were *The Aquarian Gospel of Jesus the Christ* (1908) and *Unto Thee I Grant* (1925). Emily Clark notes that core writings in the Circle 7 Koran were plagiarized from these two sources.

Ali's observation, linking African personhood to the realm of divine import, also created another theological intervention – notably the idea of religious heritability based on racial and geographical specificity. Religious faith, therefore, is braided with racial and cultural identity. Living as a Moor requires embracing the teachings of Islam, fully acknowledging in so doing, that one is concomitantly embracing his or her heritage as a son or daughter of the African diasporic community. In a word, being a good Moorish American meant embracing the historicism and facticity of one's blackness. In making this distinction, however, Ali yet again creates another fascinating iteration in his brand of African American Islamic thought that had implications for the dual realities of both African and American cultural innovations borne by African American communities. Growing into the knowledge of oneself as a true Moorish American, Ali taught – and did not in any way negate – the importance, validity, or cultural uniqueness of Christianity or any other religious tradition. Adopting what may today be referred to as interreligious pluralism, or a universalized conceptualization of the nature of religious beliefs, Ali taught that each respective nation or people, must worship under its *own* particular "vine and fig tree" (Micah 4:3-4). One 1929 editorial in *Moorish Guide*, for example, pushed Aliites to adhere to their group identity as Moors, noting that "it is the duty of every man who lives to redeem the name of his forefathers and not be herded in to a mass of weaklings [for] as long as you wear the clothes of another or live in the house of another or depend on another in any manner you are truly a slave to them…You must know the truth of your nationality and the name of your people" (Weisenfeld 2017: 44).

God's gift to the Moorish Americans was Islam, further bespeaking the appropriateness of that religion along racial lines. Ali likewise taught that Christianity was the appropriate faith for European nations – suitable for their earthly salvation – and so on along the wider spectrum of religious faith orientations and global communities. What resulted from Ali's vision was a democratic theology in the "families of all nations" in which each upheld their own distinctive faith among kith and kin – with Islam providing a divine design for pluralistic harmony, civic cooperation, interracial unity (Dew 2019: 25). Whether or not Ali and the MSTA's teachings were representative of orthodox Sunni or Shi'a Islam, at least from the standpoint of his followers, was irrelevant. What is critical, however, was that the organization itself affirmed the racial and religious legitimacy of the *Moorish American* (Clark 2013: 34). Adopting and fully embodying one's identity and sacred heritage as a Moor allowed Aliites to contest the prevailing racial and cultural terms enframing Blackness and Americanness. The consequences of this foundational and discursive shift in the psyche of Ali's followers furthermore had a mollifying effect on Aliites' sense of social boundaries and collective group affirmation, which distinguished some of the external markers of the Moorish faith-in-praxis.

Under Noble Drew Ali's guidance, Aliites, to be sure, adopted habits of dress, speech, identification, and diet that distinguished themselves as a religious community. When a new convert joined the Aliite community, he or she adopted numerous such distinctive changes denoting this conversion. After completion of the appropriate catechism(s) or religious training, new Moors would change their names – which reflected the old reality and unsuitable history mired in slave ancestry – and adopt new names and titles more in keeping with their Asiatic roots. Ali taught that the surnames Bey and El represented the "true tribal names" of Moorish Americans. These new methods of self-identification and self-fashioning inspired a sense of royalty and religious importance in the hearts, minds, and souls of the new converts (Weisenfeld 2017: 52–3). The newness of one's Moorish religio-racial identity was further reified with their membership card, bearing their new names, as well as a long inscription declaring their Moorish American identity and citizenship, honor and respect for all religious prophets, and praise to Allah (see Figure 3). Naming rituals and physical membership cards had the consequential effect of reaffirming, externally, the internal spiritual transformation wrought by following the teachings of Prophet Ali. As one Moor, Brother Blakey Bey asserted, his membership card "bore witness to his freedom from slavery, from Negro, black, colored and likewise from the fetters of Christianity" (Weisenfeld 2017: 52).

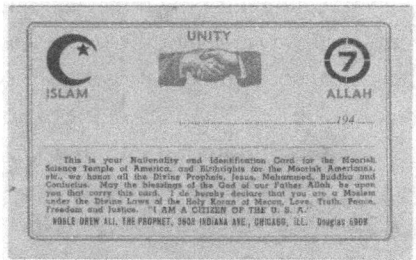

Figure 3 Identification card for the Moorish Science Temple of America. Photo permission provided by Schomburg Center for Research in Black Culture, The New York Public Library.

In many of the existing photos of Prophet Ali and his flock, perhaps reflecting the sartorial influence of Masonic garb, he and his compatriots donned turbans and fezzes, along with long robes and other headdresses for Aliite women. The choice of dress further helped distinguish the special and divine features of Aliites as Allah's chosen people, as well as served as a marker of their spiritual purity. Becoming a spiritually pure and clean nation also extended to ritualized practices involving the care and feeding of the physical body; available research on the entrepreneurial and medicinal religious work of the Moorish Americans is particularly insightful. Aside from the halal-based dietary practices widespread in Islamic teaching, which the Moors adopted, Moorish Americans also drew upon unique Asiatic bodily care practices that they then leveraged into thriving businesses whose goods and services privileged cleansing of Black bodies and souls. As Emily Clark notes, the Moorish Manufacturing Corporation, which Ali established in 1927, sold medicinal herbal teas, healing tonics, and bathing accessories and oils – all of which offered Moorish Americans a religious framework for the restoration of physical health. Ali's spiritually sanctioned products afforded accessible and alternative medical and hygienic resources for African Americans during an economic period when such services may have been denied or in short supply. Ultimately, the corporation modeled how the creative fusing of religion, health, and race were integral to Black cultural and communal identity (Clark 2013: 33).

Aliite religiosity is also noteworthy because, like that of Elijah Muhammad, Noble Drew Ali's teachings helped African Americans craft an alternate religio-racial identity that contested the restrictions of racial apartheid in American society. Yet, while Moorish Americans embraced a distinctive theology and genealogy that held that Black identity was best and most faithfully captured in Islamic teachings and Asiatic Blackness, Ali's social vision also charted a course for the Moorish Americans' cultural and political respectability in seeking equality and equal representation under the law. When Prophet Ali preached that "citizenship is salvation," he was not only operating from an assumption about the necessity of intertwining political aspirations and religious faith, but more emphatically, he was highlighting the centrality of US citizenship in the overall scope of being a good Moor. I conclude this section with a few parting comments about competing notions of citizenship, the spiritual import of this concept within the minds of Moorish Americans, and the implications of their practices thereof within the confines of American legal and racial practices of the time.

Citizenship Is Salvation: Aliites and Americanism

Nearing the end of the inscription on MSTA identification cards, it reads: "I AM A CITIZEN OF THE U.S.A." For contemporary American audiences in the twenty-first century, such a declaration may seem unremarkable. In early twentieth-century American culture, for the Moors, who were both religiously and racially minoritized, to declare their *American* identity and roots may have served to strengthen an already radicalized, insurgent positionality underscoring their dual identity as both Moor and American. In a word, Aliites sought a seamless fusion of the hallmark elements of their unique identity (re)constructions. As an indication of the complexity of the Aliite conceptualization of dual citizenship and identity, it is important to keep in mind that as Moorish Americans, Aliites rejected racial titles and categories tied to American slavery and the patterns of discrimination tied to this history, which in their view obscured true self-knowledge. Perhaps paradoxically, Prophet Ali and Moorish Americans appealed to the legal status of American citizenship and strong patriotism as a means of garnering broad-based acceptance as well as full recognition under the law, deserving full benefits, rights, and privileges thereof. Alongside the self, communal, and spiritual recovery central to Noble Drew Ali's teachings, as Dew documents, was a "divine and national project" that aimed at the creation of dual sovereignty for Moorish Americans, which was meant to emphasize racial and ethnic self-possession and *self-ownership*. On this score, Aliites pursued a sovereignty "manifest through [American] law by collective political negotiation as citizens," and then drew upon "Aliite imagination of and appeal to international law" (Dew 2019: 50).

The sovereignty project central to Aliites' navigation of their identities, place, and space as Americans reflects an effort to construct a more robust religio-racial peoplehood, which, as Sylvester Johnson notes, "promoted theologies and practices of ethnic heritage that redeemed converts from social death [in American society]" (Johnson 2010: 127). Among the insidious tools solidifying the loss of peoplehood that Ali and the MSTA's theo-political negotiation sought to correct, was the extra-legality/illegality that comprised the heart of America's praxis of racial discrimination and the partiality of its laws. As such, Aliites' pursuit of equal recognition under the law as American citizens was central to their theo-political interests and, to be sure, their self-defense against discriminatory practices. Simply put, Moorish Americans were proactive in their acceptance of the American ethos and embraced rather than recoiled from this protection as their natural birthright, even as they were aware of the "profoundly asymmetrical power relations between the state and Aliite individuals and communities" (Dew 2019: 61). Rather than distancing themselves from the American political matrix, however, Moorish Americans considered themselves part and parcel of the American experience, owing both allegiance to the American flag as well as to the flag of the Moors (Weisenfeld 2017: 221).

Evidence of Noble Drew Ali's belief in the practicalities that lay in Moorish Americans becoming politically present and viable in the mainstream is apparent in, for example, the MSTA's deep engagement with local urban politics in Chicago. Early on, Prophet Ali and the Aliites were active in Black Chicago, churning out new voters for progressive Republicans, often volunteering tirelessly for registration campaigns, as well as stumping for preferred politicians. If the Moors were to be assured representation as full citizens in American society, it was incumbent that they demonstrate power through the vote, thereby establishing themselves as a reliable and visible bloc for the Chicago Republican machine. To be sure, the MSTA was always explicit in its divine mandate to link "salvation from race-based oppression to the work of citizenship, and most specifically, to the political leverage that would result from local mobilization as a political unit" (Dew 2019: 51).

Welcoming the patronage politics adopted by figures such as Chicago mayor William Hale "Big Bill" Thompson (1869–1944), who openly courted Black votes with the promise of material recompense, Noble Drew Ali wrote in *Moorish Guide*:

> The three thousand Moslems of The Grand Temple and The West Side Temple are making ready to register every Man or Woman in order to take the lead for the various candidates whom they have been instructed to *vote* for…The Moslems will be ready. (Dew 2019: 51, original italics)

While the vote and other avenues of political proactivity as a pathway to American citizenship and equal representation under American law was a hallmark of Ali's political theology, this does not negate Ali's belief in comportment to *divine law*. That is, the quest for political sovereignty as American citizens in the thought of the MSTA must be held in a symbiotic tension with the Aliite quest for life, liberty, and happiness under divine, or *true* law – universal principles that have both eternal and temporal significance.

Divine law, as articulated by Noble Drew Ali and as embraced by the Moors, represents an innate quality that is linked to being Allah's creation.

True law, for the Aliites, is an eternal and transcendent metaphysical reality synonymous with the hallmark MSTA principles: love, truth, peace, freedom, and justice.[5] True law is the enactment and embodiment of these principles, and is furthermore, "the ultimate form of sovereignty" – encapsulating sovereignty in the legal sense, and "constituting the true grounds for instantiations of sovereignty in this world where sovereignty is multiple, relational, always negotiated" (Dew 2019: 60). Negotiating the terms of dual ideas about Moorish and American citizenship and identity also carried over into Aliite thought regarding the nature and scope of what sovereignty entailed along religious/theological/spiritual lines and how this meshed within the strictures of the nation-state. The Aliites' reliance upon the legal letter of the law (in American jurisprudence) as well as the true law, which is "innate in all humans due to their creation by Allah," allowed them a means of accessing temporal and eternal truths that emphasized and revealed their full humanity – regardless of the intricate and precarious landscape of US racial and political contexts (Dew 2019: 61).

It was through the creative dual negotiations of religious identity and citizenship on the part of Aliites that they also proffered alternative means of resisting unjust laws, making hard distinctions between the "legal" historically based ideas tied to the wielding of state power and the true, eternal ideals, thereby reimagining US society through the prism of Aliites' ideals, aspirations, and visions for the future. While Aliites clearly may have given primacy for the true, eternal law(s) grounded in their place as Allah's chosen people, sovereignty under true law still nonetheless remained part of their overall theo-political matrix, allowing for both real-time recognition as American citizens, and for future visions of the United States that privilege an expansion of the true law that grants full personhood, humanity, and citizenship to all nations and nationalities. The salvific undertones here are tied not to appeals to the restoration of one's soul by a savior, but rather, the acceptance of a globalized, multiplicity of sovereigns who are all equally subject to supreme law. Ali's democratized framework is notable for its relational impetus, and as such establishes the basis for an additional iteration in Aliite thought – namely a collectivized theology of sovereignty in the eternal sense that extends hope for disenfranchised and powerless communities who are not represented or given legal recourse for justice within the machinations of state power(s) (Dew 2019: 63).

---

[5] These attributes are listed in Act 3, Divine Constitution and By-Laws of MSTA, www.moorishamericans.com/our-laws.

Conclusion

Aliites, in their appeals for citizenship and sovereignty, did so through the language and logic of the US judicial system. While Audre Lorde famously once warned that the master's tools could never be utilized by the oppressed to construct their own spaces, clearly Noble Drew Ali was able to develop a religio-racial movement that *did* adopt American values that aligned with those of the MSTA and Aliite religious orientations. In doing so, he created a theological and political foundation for African American converts who both sought recourse against the anti-Black beliefs and praxis central to American life, yet desired to maintain a stake in the system of rights assured to them under the law and by virtue of their natural birthright. Adopting American social, legal, and governmental norms as central to their identity as a religious body and, furthermore, contextualizing these within the orbit of their religious and theological motivations, indicates the expanse of Aliites' belief in the apparatus of the American experiment. Even as the rule of law underscoring the US nation-state is always already a reflection of White supremacy and the reification of White colonial empire, in which Black and Brown bodies are always at a deficit, Aliites carved for themselves another way forward in their efforts to survive with some semblance of integrity and dignity intact – all while drawing upon discourses and intellectual categories seemingly ill-suited for the advance of a Black religio-racial community.

In "The Rise of the Black Ethnics: The Ethnic Turn in Black Religions," Sylvester Johnson opines that

> ethnicity is first and foremost a discourse, a thoroughly historical construction [that] reflects worldly interests fundamentally rooted in the anxieties over membership in an American nation-state whose primordial content and scope has persistently been inscribed through exclusive white racial subjectivity. (Johnson 2010: 127)

One of the fascinating aspects, historically speaking, of religio-racial organizations is the way their members constructed alternative framings of the import and significance of racial identity and at the same time transplant those into religious orientations and belief structures that hinged upon notions of the sacred, spirituality, and hopes tied to more vibrant futures. In the case of the Aliites, as Johnson notes, creating a new vision of Black-identity-as-Moorish illustrates primarily an ideological and discursive boundlessness – a space of ontological freedom. That is, reorienting religion and race against the backdrop of historical, social, legal, and political restrictions reveals an artfulness – a creative disregard for what "is" – in favor of what could and should be. For the Aliites, this about-face on the construct of religion (specifically of the Islamic persuasion) and race (rejection of Black/Negro in favor of Moorish/Asiatic) provided new existential and even legalistic sites through which Noble Drew Ali and his followers could imagine and aspire to new heights of human personhood on the basis of a renewed understanding of citizenship and sovereignty on American soil.

4 Holy Race(less) Angels: Father Divine and the International Peace Mission Movement

It may appear odd to refer to Father Divine's Peace Mission (PM) as a "Black" religious movement. While the PM founder, Father Divine (1876–1965), was in fact a Black man with roots in the southern United States, and most of his followers were African Americans, the PM collectively was interracial, marked by a broad contingency of White members – a feat no doubt remarkable for Depression-era America, when its membership began to swell. Even as the PM was and remains an interracial religious community, that its messianic leader was an African American man is worthy of our critical analysis. But this notwithstanding, what does it mean that Divine's teachings and theology hinged upon not the centralizing or restoration of racial identity, but rather, its *erasure* as a diminishment of one's spiritual purity and accentuation of the divine spirit within. I hold no easy answers here regarding the categorization of the PM movement as a Black religious movement. Despite this, I deem it necessary to hold the specter of non-racialism in tension with Divine's teachings and the impact on PM theology and correlated social beliefs and practices.

At the very least, we may assert with confidence that PM doctrines of race were in themselves unique, and proved to be radical because they inaugurated an alternative telos for conceptualizations of religio-racial identity that allowed both Blacks *and* Whites to repurpose and reenvision community and cultural belonging – a belonging not tied to phenotype, caste, or class, but rather, to a heightened religiosity and shared set of commitments grounded in alignment with the word and will of Father Divine, New Thought philosophy, and countercultural arrangements of place and space that harkened to an imagined but unrealized post-Civil Rights American society unburdened by the restrictions of racial and sexual hierarchies. In place of these hierarchies, which determined, largely, the ebb and flow of American social and political orders, PM communities adopted a deracialized identity construct – one in which social restrictions tied to "White," "Black," "Negro," or "colored," were considered an obscene deviation from true identity as a conduit for divine authority and personhood. In its place, PM members aligned themselves with Father Divine's charismatic teachings, in which he was embraced as God personified and they lived as his righteous angels[6] in perfect unity – exemplifying before the world what true community could entail despite the restriction of race and sex dichotomies, as well as economic precarity.

God Dwells Within: Father Divine and New Thought

I am here with you all personally for your own personal good and to appease your human mortal concept concerning Me, and your fears, but, with or without the Personal Presence, I will rule millions of homes and houses, for I AM DIVINE, and that is not merely a word, it is a Power.

Father Divine, November 1931 (Watts 1992: 72)

When Father Divine made the above declaration, citing his divine authority and deeming it "a Power," this was no mere dramatic assertion. Rather, it affirmed the intrinsic power of verbalizing and believing in one's personal and spiritual *self*-affirmation. His word and will were in perfect alignment and occasioned the foundation for his religious authority and power. As we will see, however, Divine's belief in the power of positive self-affirmation and self-esteem – which established spiritual and physical perfection – was adopted from longstanding philosophical discourses tied to New Thought religious ideology, which he encountered in his pre-PM ministry experiences as an itinerant urban storefront pastor in Baltimore, Maryland. Tracing Father Divine's family ties and background prior to the establishment of the PM is difficult, in part due to his recalcitrance to acknowledge flesh and blood family, along with the PM movement's practice of disregarding (earthly) familial records, sometimes renouncing them entirely. Divine, also known as "Major Jealous Father Divine," according to some historians, was born George Baker Jr., in May 1879. Contemporary biographers and a few periodicals have linked his birthplace to coastal Georgia and to North Carolina. Jill Watts's history of Divine's life, theological development, and the larger movement relies upon census data locating an appropriately aged "George Baker Jr." born in Rockville, Maryland,[7] in an African American neighborhood known as

---

[6] PM followers were also known as "Divinites."
[7] It also necessary to note that remaining members of Peace Mission do not agree with Watts's conclusions about Father Divine's ancestry, or her interpretation of the census data about the Baker family.

Monkey's Run (Watts 1992). The mysteries surrounding Divine's actual birth no doubt contributed to the aura surrounding his perceived divinity among his followers.

To properly contextualize the religious and theological commitments of the PM and the teachings of Father Divine, one must begin with his early ministry, specifically his foray into freethought traditions prior to his founding the PM. Watts notes that Divine's early religious instruction as a child was largely tied to Black Methodism, along with some exposure to the Catholicism of his mother, Nancy. With the African American Jerusalem Methodist Church in Rockville, Maryland, the Baker family, like so many other families in the years immediately after slavery, sought respite through independent church participation and leadership in response to the bureaucracy and restrictiveness of local White congregations. As a child, Father Divine was largely immersed in church life, regularly attending Sunday school, prayer meetings, and Bible studies. Notably, however, the Black Methodist congregation offered psychological protection for Black families against the dehumanizing realities of both White surveillance and White patronization that stemmed from their social and structural overreach – a carryover from the American slave state (Watts 1992: 11). In terms of polity, or organizational structure, it is worth noting that the Methodist church allowed for relatively open and fluid opportunities for religious leadership and was among the most prominent religious denominations that courted the membership of African Americans during the first and second Great Awakening periods. In addition to this, the early development of Divine's religious and theological sensibilities were also impacted by the "open heart" spirituality of Methodism – which required not stringent doctrinal training or extended catechesis, but only sincerity of spirit and a desire for spiritual and social transformation.

These early experiences of spiritual formation established fertile ground in the recesses of Divine's religious imagination, fostering an openness to alternate visions of the world and the operation of his faith therein. Along with other African Americans during the Great Migration period, Divine sought economic and spiritual relief in larger urban cities, and found himself in the storefront churches of Baltimore, which continued to nurture and strengthen his religious commitments while broadening his spirituality. Divine's adulthood years in Baltimore were particularly formative; as it was during this time that his eclectic religious worldview was exposed to New Thought discourse, which would arguably be the central philosophical worldview that characterized the eventual teachings central to PM theology and its later growth into New York and Pennsylvania. Drawing upon elements of Catholicism, the Black Church, Methodism, and the storefront traditions, Divine was able to craft an attractive syncretistic brand of theology that was made more appealing with the juxtaposition of New Thought philosophy (Watts 1992: 21).

Featuring a theological lineage with roots in mid-nineteenth-century New England and shaped by philosophical and religious thinkers such as mystic Charles Fillmore (1854–1948), mentalist, spiritual writer, and healer Phineas Parker Quimby (1802–1866), Pentecostal faith healer William J. Seymour (1870–1922), and Christian Science founder, Mary Baker Eddy (1821–1910), New Thought philosophy holds that one's outward, external being is shaped by positive self-thought. As an example, Father Divine was known to regularly utter a known phrase in many of his sermons and religious teachings: "Accentuate the Positive!" While you and I may relegate this phrase to popular songs in American culture,[8] for Divine it was indicative of a call to action and embodied a living theology of mental prowess meant to be practiced in the everyday and the mundane. That is, what Divine taught was akin to "mind over matter" – or, rather, that the state of the mind shapes matters that impact and frame the totality of the human condition, including its fortunes and foibles.

New Thought ideology maintains that one's individual mindset has the power to impact material reality; that a positive, affirmational psychology will reap grand benefits in one's material condition. According to R. Marie Griffith, while the early iterations of New Thought discourses underwent some gradual definitional shifts among its proponents through the nineteenth century, it came to encapsulate the belief that one could "align oneself with the rational cosmic force commonly referred to as Mind, All-Supply, or Universal Spirit and thereby attract to oneself the abundance that had once seemed unattainable" (Griffith 2001: 124). A few observations are notable on this point. New Thought ideology nestles an agential, proactive quality that places the onus of spiritual growth and spiritual purity into the hands the discerning believer. This removes the necessity of relying upon an external salvific figure. Rather, one's saving grace is entirely self-contained and tied to his or her powers of positive self-regard. It is also interesting that proper state of mind is further linked, per Griffith, to an explicit attraction to *abundance*, which could be spiritual or material. The latter emphasis regarding material abundance,

---

[8] Several vocalists, including Aretha Franklin, Bing Crosby, and Perry Como, have covered the song, "Accentuate the Positive ("Ac-Cent-Tchu-Ate the Positive")," but it was the publicity agent of songwriter and singer Johnny Mercer, who heard this phrasing during one of Divine's sermons and ultimately pitched the idea to Mercer for recording.

and specifically the belief that positive thinking yields positive outcomes, could be an early expression of what we know today as "prosperity" theology, which teaches that material wealth and physical health is God's will and directly tied to the strength of one's articulated faith (Bowler 2013). Prosperity theology is popular among charismatic Christian communities and furthermore highlighted in the preaching and teaching of noted televangelists such as Creflo Dollar, Joel Osteen, and Paula White. It seems philosophically linked to the New Thought paradigms that influenced Divine's theology, which held that all people have the capacity for spiritual purity within.

Father Divine taught his followers to see God's spirit, which was his spirit, in all matters – and further, to locate and accentuate the divine within themselves. This theological interpretation seems premised upon 1 Corinthians 3:16 (NIV): "Don't you know that you yourselves are God's temple and that God's Spirit dwells in your midst?" In Father Divine's thinking, godliness and divinity were not ethereal principles divorced from the material realm, but rather, were "here and now" in the recesses of human history and material experience. In addition to teaching that he was God in a physical body, Divine aroused the followers of his movement with his teaching that all possessed the spirit of God, his spirit, within themselves. And because the spirit of God was found in all persons, arbitrary distinctions tied to race, sex, gender, or socioeconomic status were irrelevant, despite prevailing social norms (Clark and Stoddard 2019: 113). There are at least two interventions in which Divine's New Thought theology was significant for the PM movement: (1) offering an organic theodicy of self-help as the correction to negative thinking and (2) providing a theological justification for the dismantling of American racialization.

In linking the proactive quality of Divine's New Thought paradigm to theodicy specifically, I am calling attention to the varied modes of human suffering – which here are read as spiritually devastating evils – reconciled through Divine's insistence upon positive faith(ful) thinking meant to effectively thwart and/or mitigate the severity of human frailties. One of the central components of Divine's unique brand of New Thought was its emphasis on anti-materiality – detachment from the mortal realm and earthly afflictions, including sickness, disease, and other personal ailments. Health and well-being were directly influenced by mindset and individual psychology. As Weisenfeld asserts:

> The health and healing Divine offered his followers were not to be sought through physical means… Divine emphasized that he did not

heal through his presence or physical touch, but that followers themselves effected healing by achieving the right state of spirit and mind in concert with his spirit and mind. (Weisenfeld 2017: 152)

Not only was physical health a manifestation of a healthy psychology; one's fortune or misfortune was impacted as well. The personal correspondence between Divine and his followers illustrates the alternative healing practices PM members sought by aligning themselves with the will, spirit, and mindset of Father Divine. Writing to the PM's publication *Spoken Word* in 1936, new convert Simon Peter claimed that Divine appeared to him in a vision, but he was ignorant of who Divine was until a fellow member revealed that Divine was "the second Christ." After reaching out to Divine, Peter then "became convinced of his divinity and claimed that his cancer, eye disease, and heart disease had been cured as a result of aligning his mind with Divine's. 'My body is the Temple of God, Father Divine!' he declared" (Weisenfeld 2017: 152).

These and other healing testimonies reveal the extent to which PM members not only sought recourse through religion for physical health concerns but also reveals the context for the emergence of a theology/theodicy of self-help in response to personal traumas and tragedies. If misfortune befell the fellow kingdom dwellers in the PM, Divine encouraged them to retrace and interrogate disconnects within the mind as the spiritual culprit. It was necessary to correct all such mental and psychic ruptures unlinked from Divine's will or inappropriately tethered to mortal desires/weaknesses in the form of doubt, in lieu of spiritual strength as vested by true faith. By teaching that one's spiritual and physical state was tied to faith and mental fortitude and situated within a spiritual alignment with Divine, PM followers crafted an effective psycho-spiritual prophylactic that enabled them to navigate the varied ills, physical or social, that shaped their experiences in Depression-era American society and beyond. As one Brooklyn resident testified after being cared for following a stroke by PM follower Miss P. Love, "Miss Love tells me that for my asking [to be healed by Father Divine] you will heal me inwardly so I shall not be sick again." Divine replied:

> [As] you cast mammon out of your life by casting the tendencies of Adam, of race division, of greed, of selfishness and every other mortal expression of man, from your consciousness, you will give God's Grace, Health, and Strength free access to express within you…lifting you up from your ailment and complaint. (Weisenfeld 2017: 153)

The impact of New Thought on Divine's racial doctrines resulted in very radical prescriptions for Jim Crow societies in America, both in the north and in the south. To restate, Divine taught that one's internal psychology impacted physical and spiritual being. He also taught that attachment to the mortal, the earthly, and the mundane realms resulted in spiritual and physical maladies, as it hinged upon a fixation with this-worldliness and not the realm of God's spirit. Notably, this feature of Divine's racial doctrine stipulated that racialized categories, and reliance upon them, illustrates ongoing worldly attachment. Because PM members "strove to detach themselves from mortal life in hopes of achieving eternal life in the Kingdom of God on earth," racial stigmas and qualifications represented key fixtures of the worldly realm that kept them from fully linking with Divine's spirit (Weisenfeld 2017: 197). For Father Divine and his followers, racial categories lacked any real substance. The categories Black, White, and Negro, for example, were false signifiers that obscured rather than clarified the true nature of a person. As an example, Arthur Huff Fauset's landmark ethnographic study, *Black Gods of the Metropolis* notes that Divine so held to the doctrine of racelessness that he went as far as forbidding the use of racial terms even in written form. In published writings, for example, the PM used linguistic strategies, adopting W---- for White, and C---- for Colored (Fauset 2002: 61). This feature of Divine's teachings had the consequence of introducing a novel understanding of race relations that was foreign to American communities of his time, and in some ways, was a foreshadowing of the idealized "color blindness" often heralded by post-1960s Civil Rights progressivism.

It is also important to keep in mind the interracialism that characterized PM social arrangements. For Black PM members, what Divine taught was viewed as liberation from the constraints of the racial contract designating their inferiority. As one member put it, Divine was to be praised "for breaking up discrimination, for making [African Americans] lose [their] identity" (which presumably was overdetermined by racial restrictions) (Weisenfeld 2017: 80). He and his followers' "nonracial approach underscored members' belief in the spiritually destructive consequences of investing skin color with meaning attached to racial hierarchy" (Weisenfeld 2017: 116). To be sure, a nuanced read of Divine's views on race reveals moments of contradiction, but these views evolved over time as he became more attuned to the social situation confronting African Americans within the discriminatory infrastructures of America.[9]

---

[9] Father Divine, "GOD, Through His Condescension, Always Did Come in the Most Insignificant Expression," June 14, 1938, http://peacemission.info/sermons-by-father-divine/god-through-his-condescension-always-did-come-in-the-most-insignificant-expression/.

For Divine himself, his self-conception was that of God in a physical body – a body that perhaps appeared to the outside world as Black, balding, and of short stature. As he noted to the famed Harlem Renaissance writer Claude McKay: "I have no color conception of myself. If I were representing race or creed or color or nation, I would be limited in my conception of the universal. I would not be as I am, omnipotent" (Weisenfeld 2017: 80). For Divine and his followers, his was a raceless body, that, while phenotypically Black, ultimately did not embody the racial value judgments embraced by wider, and Whiter, America. Racism, and its corresponding colorism, as Divine taught, was all a projection of negative thinking, which was the underpinning of all social divisiveness in America.

Pursuing a train of thought foreshadowing White, evangelical views on the race problem later in the twenty-first century, Divine believed that racism was a spiritual and psychological problem, rather than institutional, and as such, could largely be resolved based on the individual's personal efforts.[10] On this score, there are points in Divine's early ministry in which he seems to blame the racial plight of African Americans squarely on their shoulders, suggesting that their vulnerabilities stemmed not from the racial apartheid instituted by Whites, but from African Americans internalizing and manifesting the negative beliefs that debased them (Watts 1992: 89). Seeking to disassociate himself from the literal products of this negative racialized thinking, Divine once announced during a meeting: "The other night someone got up and said there were lots of c[olored] people from New Orleans [present]…I don't care anything about c[olored] people. I haven't them in me…[and] cast them out of my consciousness and do not allow them to exist there" (Watts 1992: 89).

Divine's imprisonment stemming from White backlash to his growing, and interracial, ministries served to provide an opportunity to give his racial doctrines added nuance. Prior to relocating the PM headquarters to Harlem, from 1919 to 1931 Divine and his early disciples operated out of the resort town of Sayville in Long Island, New York in a home on 72 Macon Street, becoming the first local Black homeowner. Incensed by their new neighbors, as well as the weekly high-spirited integrated worship services and communion banquets that led to street congestion from parked cars, White Sayville residents bitterly complained for years until

---

[10] My observation here is largely in reference to the racialization thesis and the ethnographic studies on White evangelicals featured within Michael O. Emerson and Christian Smith's *Divided by Faith: Evangelical Religion and the Problem of Race in America* (New York: Oxford University Press, 2001).

local police arrested Divine for disturbing the peace on May 8, 1931. While Divine was in prison, he devoted much of his time to personal reflection on the scope of his ministry and remained attuned to contemporary affairs – notably the case involving the Scottsboro Nine, in which innocent Black youths were falsely accused of the rape of two White women.

Watts cites Divine's experiences of arrest and his burgeoning sociopolitical consciousness of the material implications of race – along with New Thought discourses – as being consequential for a shift in the tone of his sermons toward pressing social concerns. Ultimately, Divine's "incarceration allowed him to think more about earthly concerns and it revitalized his theology" by making him more responsive to worldly affairs as well as strengthening his understanding of the material realities that shaped African American experiences within the judicial system. Divine continued to preach self-help through positive thinking and the shunning of negative race-based ideology, a conservative approach by both past and present standards. His imprisonment nonetheless gave him additional interpretive tools that expanded his appreciation for America's legal system and its potential to rid itself of the "human errors" of spirit and thought that prevented the full embrace of the "fundamental principle" of the Kingdom of God (Watts 1992: 100–1).

Finally, that White PM members adopted Divine's racial views is not unremarkable. On one level, this surely confirms Father Divine's charisma, whose presence and aura commanded reverence and attention from both admirer and critic alike, all of which exploded racial lines. When PM follower Lovely Young was interviewed by a Los Angeles reporter, she took umbrage at the "newspaper's characterization of her as 'a white secretary' in Father Divine's movement." Young's response: "I am not a white secretary because I recognize no race, class, color, or creed, but am a child of the Resurrection, born again!" (Weisenfeld 2017: 80). It is arguable that Divine's presence and the belief in his divinity as the perfection of God's spirit was a boon to the beleaguered hopes and aspirations of African American followers, as this was a tangible benefit to both their psychic health and their capacity for spiritual restoration despite the throes of American racism and economic blight. But, what specifically did White PM members gain from nonracial thought?

Whites who adopted Father Divine's theology and his prescriptions for race did so at the expense of their own hold on the reigns of racial privilege and the trappings of hierarchy under which they thrived. To put the matter another way, Divine's emphasis on racial erasure and eschewing the idea of race as a marker of one's value, dignity, or personhood, dismantled the common meta-assumptions underscoring the character of American social worlds, as well as the assumptions of (White) humanity and (non-White) inhumanity. Divine's PM movement upended, to a limited degree, centuries of race-based discourses and ontic designations that operationalized the social and anthropic norms of the Western world. And more pointedly, he was able to garner significant acceptance from American Whites while doing so – prompting their turn from the racial hierarchical system that propped up their power, prestige, and privileges. To circle back to Divine's charisma, Sweet Angel (formerly Edna Rose Ritchings), also known as Mother Divine, and who was Father Divine's second wife, suggested that it was purely the power of his spirit that justified his spiritual accomplishments across racial lines. As she revealed to an interviewer: "God coming in that expression…he didn't have anything but his own holy spirit and mind to work with…and he didn't have any ancestors that he could look to, to give him any credibility; he had nothing. So it took God to do what he did do."[11]

Father Divine was able to create an interracial coalition in his ministry – defying the social conventions and expectations of his time and establishing a renewed path toward integrated communalism prior to the great shifts of the Civil Rights era. Roger Klaus, another White follower of Father Divine observed: "The people here. .are all races, creeds, and colors, and this is God's family – the birthplace of the Kingdom of God on Earth."[12] It may be that the PM movement gave receptive Whites a renewed hope in the possibility of a natural symbiosis between the races, driven not by governmental intervention or social engineering, but through an organic religious and spiritual means grounded in the shared belief in Father Divine's teachings. The raceless identity formation Divine espoused may have been aimed at African American followers, but the larger contribution of the PM movement socially coincides with its confrontation and challenge to American racial hierarchies and his invitation to both Blacks and Whites to reject racial categorization as an affront to true community.

Angelic Heavens: Race, Sex, and Community in the Peace Mission Movement

In a devotional collage made by a follower of Father Divine, the image that adorns the card features decorative wreathing around the borders, and at the center is the drawing of a human eye, with a picture of Father

---

[11] "Father Divine: A Case Study in Charisma," www.youtube.com/watch?v=hG09gRuBVhE&t=51s.

[12] "Father's Kingdom," www.youtube.com/watch?v=rqOL09kfPow.

Divine's face in the pupil. Around the eye, an inscription reads, "I Have Eyes Only For You!" (Weisenfeld 2017: 187) Such was the artistic expression of a devoted follower seeking the approval and favor of Father Divine. What is fascinating about this image and the devotion of its creator, is the relational implication – an effective example that allows for additional commentary upon another feature of the identity markers self-selected by PM members, and which frames the communal arrangements of PM ministry sites. The unnamed artist of this collage, saw himself or herself as one of Father Divine's children: an *angel*. In most Christian theological traditions, angels are believed to be messengers from God, who are also tasked with intervening in human affairs for multiple purposes, including protection and guidance. For our purposes, the self-designation of PM members as angels can be read in one light as addressing their desire to reclaim identities unbound by the negativity of racial caste/class and color. More importantly, angelic as a description of their human personhood also substantiates a higher spiritual praxis that delineates the standard for personal conduct and arrangements of space and place for PM members.

The rigid restrictions of Divine's moral and ethical standards befitting PM communities necessitated rarified, set-apart space in which angels could live according to their principles and Divine's teachings. Of the PM members' "angelic life," Weisenfeld observes:

> For members of Father Divine's Peace Mission, embrace of a raceless identity as children of God also entailed rejection of sex, marriage, and emotional and material connections to family. Everything about members' lives prior to accepting the divinity of Father Divine had to be left behind because these tied them to what he characterized as mortal negativity and prevented them from aligning their minds with his spirit and consciousness. (Weisenfeld 2017: 182–3)

What emerges from this description of PM social norms and communal choices immediately invokes notions of dualism – a denial of the features of materiality and the flesh, in preference for spirituality. Angelic life among PM communities emphasized absolute devotion to Father Divine and called for the enactment of that devotion through the denial of racial identity and countercultural living arrangements. On some level, Divine's teaching to reject the members' "old" lives and their attachment to thinking and acting in accordance with "mortal negativity" seems linked to Jesus' declaration in Luke 14:26: "If anyone comes to me and does not hate father and mother, wife and children, brothers and sisters – yes, even their own life – such a person cannot be my disciple" (NIV). In modeling his expectations for discipleship after Christ, as the perfected spirit of

God, Father Divine compelled his followers to draw a line in the sand regarding the intensity of their devotion to him – to pick a side. In doing so, the most devoted of his followers renounced their worldly attachments and took up their own individual crosses to bear by following Divine and living in PM enclaves.

PM communes were ministry sites, often referred to as "Heavens," in which Angels could live among one another according to Divine's ordained principles. The International PM's modesty code included restrictions against smoking, alcoholic beverages, obscenities/vulgarities and undue mixing of the sexes. One of the bitter criticisms from outsiders and critics of the movement, along with defectors who eventually broke with Divine's teachings, was that it split whole families apart and, in some cases, even left some children orphaned by parents who abandoned them after converting to Divine's movement. On the nature of the specific appeal that Divine had, and the pull on so many people in this way, it is vital to hold this fact in tension with what Divine taught about worldly attachment. Attachment to the material realm was an obstacle to spiritual purity and depth and rendered one susceptible to an impotence of faith that inevitably threatened one's health and well-being and their material flourishing. To be sure, however, not all PM followers remained convinced of this theology of spiritual damnation wrought by worldly attachment. Such was the case of PM members James Alladice and Beulah Prescott, who met and married, and then promptly left the movement in 1939 – feeling restricted by Divine's teachings and ignoring the warnings that such unions would invite wrath and bring about their deaths (Weisenfeld 2017: 188).

The American Heavens that housed Divine's Angels were sex segregated and functioned under the absolute laws of celibacy. While many of Divine's secretarial staff who helped with running his ministry and other organizational endeavors were comprised of women, Divine decreed that the living arrangements among women and men should be separate – with the sexes living on alternate floors in each building. Divine further reinforced the doctrine of celibacy by establishing varied gender religious orders: The (Real True) Rosebuds, designating the women who pledged absolute virginity and had "hearts where Christ alone is heard;" the Lily-Buds, featuring women "redeemed from carnality" through holy and clean living; and finally, the Crusaders, a men's coalition likewise emphasizing pure behavior and moral conduct as the conduit for establishing the Kingdom of God on earth (Weisenfeld 2017: 188). It is worth noting that Divine seemed especially emphatic regarding the Rosebuds and virginal womanhood as the fundamental marker of virtue. Weisenfeld correlates

Divine's decision to establish sex-based religious orders within the PM as strategic – namely as a response to skeptical observers who questioned wide adherence to celibacy among the Angels, and in response to some of the sexual scandals that rocked the PM movement. This included the 1937 conviction of White PM member John Wuest Hunt, who violated the Mann Act by transporting an underage woman across state lines for the purposes of sexual congress.

Divine's prescriptions for sexual segregation and celibacy also faced another interpretive challenge for both PM members and critics – in this case because Divine had two wives.[13] The first was a Black woman named Penninah, whom he married during his early years in New York. After Penninah's death – and the conspicuous reluctance to acknowledge her illness and death publicly – Father Divine made waves by marrying his second wife, a 21-year-old White, Canadian woman, Edna Rose Ritchings, in 1946 (see Figure 4). Divine considered both marriages to be spiritual unions, based more on companionship, mutual respect, and reverence toward himself, rather than romantic and/or carnal attraction, which served as an "integral part of his broader work to purify the world and establish a kingdom characterized by the absence of racial divisions" (Weisenfeld 2017: 195).

While living arrangements of the PM members in their varied Heavens did elicit curiosity and scorn from both orthodox religious communities

Figure 4 Father Divine and his second wife, Mother Divine (Edna Rose Ritchings). Photo permission provided by Temple University Libraries Digital Collections.

---

[13] Both of the women were known, respectively, as Mother Divine in their spiritual marriages to Father Divine.

and the casual observer, PM communities were also well known, particularly during the years in Harlem at the height of the Great Depression, for their lavish Holy Communion banquets that would feed hundreds, if not thousands on a weekly basis. Often, these services were an introduction to the PM movement as well as to the theology and preaching of Father Divine, who, when present, delivered a sermon that was later transcribed and published in the standard PM periodicals, *Spoken Word* and *New Day*. One woman who attended Communion in 1948 wrote to Divine about her experience: "Father I ate at the feast until I could hold no more. I've never in my life seen so much to eat and drink, its [sic] most wonderful" (Weisenfeld 2017: 148).

These communion services had multiple impacts on the followers and others who participated. Given the social context of the Great Depression, in which these banquets occurred, it is worth noting that feeding broad swaths of the urban poor was a form of social relief against the backdrop of destitution and the hope-killing despair of poverty. Furthermore, this relief to which the Angels were so central, was a proactive venture in which the larger movement was able to pool its resources, resulting in the establishment of PM-run groceries, delicatessens, restaurants, and even farmland in Ulster County, New York. These investments and resources were then rechanneled back into the PM Heavens and the surrounding districts to be utilized for cost-effective food preparation and the offering of other goods and services. More critically, the decade during the 1930s was a time marked by great food insecurity, whence even social welfare organizations and food banks had difficulty assisting the larger population. That Father Divine, lacking a government grant or a political machine, could provide a seemingly endless spread of hearty meals to starving people, astonished his contemporaries and likely intensified his early recognition of the need to leverage his religious faith to social advancement. As he declared during a 1932 Easter communion service: "I preach Christ not only in word, but in deed and action. What I have to offer is only an outward expression of a percent of the limitless blessings I have in the store house for you" (Watts 1992: 91). Father Divine's ministry, through the Holy Communion feasts, served two ends: they provided material and spiritual sustenance for both bodies and souls – restoring and reviving the hopes of many during times of despair and lack. Further, the feasts bolstered Divine's eminence as a God of bounty and blessing who was able to provide material and spiritual abundance to all who accepted his spirit and consciousness through faith.

Conclusion

PM interviewees in Fauset's study were adamant that the "true followers of Father Divine will never die," for death "is the last weakness which the faithful are to overcome" (Fauset 2002: 63). In response to the illness and eventual death of his first wife, Penninah, Divine had to refine his doctrine of spiritual and physical immortality as tied to depth of faith, which he did, by suggesting that Penninah's spirit was reincarnated in the form of his second wife, a belief that has remained constant into the present day. Remaining PM Angels do not believe Father Divine died in 1965 at age 89. God cannot die. Rather, Father Divine's spirit simply left his earthly vessel. Confident in this spiritual truth, current PM members carry on Divine's hope for a raceless society governed under the plan of righteousness in which positive self-affirmation and an abiding faith corrects the spiritual and social maladies that destroy human personhood and communal life. A few remaining members still maintain Divine's mansion and his *Shrine to Life* at Woodmont in Gladwyne, Pennsylvania; the rest are scattered in the few surviving PM Heavens.

As a religio-racial movement, Father Divine's International PM Movement offered members a theology and social platform emphasizing the denial of race as the determining feature of a person or community's value. Unencumbered with the proverbial walls that impacted the social and racial ills dismantling community and spiritual fulfillment in the broader public, PM members were afforded renewed space through which they were free to shape their own destinies among like-minded people, providing spiritual, material, and communal succor that was sorely anemic in American society. Along the way, Divine and his Angels provided material sustenance for the soul and body through his savvy entrepreneurial sense, as evident in the PM movement's business ventures that offered goods and services throughout New York City and Philadelphia during times of great scarcity, which Divine managed through a well-organized bureaucratic structure.

Divine was recognized as a legitimate forebear for African Americans' civil rights, even as he had no invested racial consciousness and went to great lengths to reject racial categories and disassociate them from any significant value in the self-conception of his followers. Moreover, Divine inaugurated a way of speaking, being, and doing that was meant to recreate a new sense of purpose and direction for his followers – one that in many ways was foreign to the larger social and racial habitus in early-mid twentieth-century America. Following the New Thought orientations on which much of his ministry, theology, and philosophical foundations were based, Divine was able to craft a new religious orientation that instilled within PM members an agency and guardianship over their lives and destinies, in this world and in the spiritual realm.

The safety and comfort of PM Heavens provided a respite – a reprieve from the "business-as-usual" worldliness of the mundane and the secular – even as these Heavens and their angels were lodged within its frame. In one manner, however, the PM Heavens that Father Divine directed were situated, within the religious imaginations of his followers, *above* their worldly counterparts, essentially rendering their communities spiritually above reproach and holier than their immediate contexts. This had the twin effect(s) of both a psychological edge, rooted in their shared beliefs about the purity and maintenance of their convictions, and a sense of societal isolation – even in the middle of the city. Today, there are only a handful of aging PM followers, no doubt due to the movement's inflexible teachings on celibacy and the denial of earthly familial connection. It is hard to imagine the movement reaching its impressive membership numbers during the early twentieth century, but what is apparent is the seriousness with which the remaining PM members have committed themselves to maintaining Father Divine's theology and its ties to contemporary race relations.

Peace Mission Holy Communion feasts are still run by surviving Angels at a few PM extension sites. Without fail, and through song and adorations of praise, these members show reverence to Father Divine, with his picture gracing every banquet hall in a small shrine. At each banquet table, an empty seat and a full plate of food is preserved, for Father Divine is present in spirit, and each PM member acknowledges and addresses his presence. While Father Divine's physical body has departed, his followers' preservation of his felt spiritual presence serves as stark reminder of the steadfast influence his teachings have had on those who have found renewed identity and belonging in Heaven.

Conclusion – Reading Blackness Rightly: The Impact of New Religious Movements on Black Selfhood

Returning to *Wayward Lives, Beautiful Experiments*, where this Element began, Saidiya Hartman offers an examination of the sexualities, intimate lives, and histories of early twentieth-century Black women throughout New York and Philadelphia – crafting a counternarrative that contests the efforts to punish and confine these communities and diminish their complete agency and autonomy. These "wayward" women, Hartman notes, were so, because of their capacity for creative disregard for the rigidities of their societal context. To be wayward demands an embrace of "the untiring practice of trying to live when you were never meant to survive" (Hartman 2019: 228). The portrait that emerges from Hartman's study is one of women who were radical in their strident safeguarding of the hope of full humanity and undeterred sexual agency. These women, as sexually and racially minoritized and subordinated, lived "against the grain" – that is, in manners that challenged the norms and standards dictating their personal lives. While Hartman's work centralizes the lives of Black queer women, her conceptualization of waywardness offers an appropriate context that can be transplanted toward our understanding of Black religious movements.

Students of African American religions may properly think of the communities, historical actors, and religious orientations reviewed in this Element as, perhaps, "wayward" religiosities that trouble the landscape(s) of popular theoretical considerations of Black religious meaning-making in America and abroad. In noting this, of course, one must also consider how contemporary theorizations of religion, and Black religion in particular, prompt interpretive tensions that necessitate a shift in hermeneutical approach. Dianne M. Stewart and Tracey E. Hucks highlight many of these tensions for our consideration in their groundbreaking 2013 article, "Africana Religious Studies: Toward a Transdisciplinary Agenda in an Emerging Field," which expands theoretical and methodological frameworks in the landscape of Africana religious thought. Through attention to the broad complexities of both the continent of Africa as well as the varied expressions of African-derived religious heritages that shape contemporary Black religious communities, Stewart and Hucks spotlight the need for interpretive approaches in the study of (Black) religion that safeguard the uniqueness and integrity of the spiritual lives and agency of African-descended communities across the diaspora (Stewart and Hucks 2013).[14] Yet, another tension is grounded in the form of a foundational challenge to Black religious studies, which J. Kameron Carter explores in *The Anarchy of Black Religion*. What we deem religious cannot be lodged singularly in the study of traditions, histories, institutions, or cultic orders. In Carter's view, if we are to take seriously the manner(s) in which religion

---

[14] To be sure, however, Stewart and Hucks's focus in this article gives particular attention to religious scholarship on African traditions, cultures, and communities in the Americas and the Caribbean.

provides an apparatus for the material arrangements of societies and cultures, including those in which the constructs of race are central, it is critical to reframe our understanding of religion, namely its capaciousness for "structuring imagination of matter and culture" (Carter 2023: 4).

What I glean from Carter is the need to tarry with recasting the terms for interpreting Black religion and Black religiosity. This observation implicates the agency and integrity of Black religious communities, including the communities examined in this Element. In the vein of Hartman's conceptualization of the wayward as an expression of Black women's contestation against racial and gendered norms, we may also view NBRMs as alternate religio-racial frameworks of destabilization, which Carter discusses as the "an-archic" quality of Black religion. Black religions and Black religious actors contest the rules – the enframements "at the forefront of [White racial and intellectual] empire's new terms of cultural order and knowing" (Carter 2023: 8). In further calling for a uniquely "Black study of religion," Carter also endeavors to disclose how religion "proper," that is, as part of the machinery of White racial empire, invents and reinvents the category of "the human," whence "human" emerges as a religiopolitical construct that functions as a buffering agent binding some human groups over against others (Carter 2023: 15–16). In shifting gears a bit, I'd like to conclude by engaging Carter's insights further as a segue toward reading Blackness and Black religious movements anew in light of the disruptive and creative webs of meaning-making and matter-making that shape the interventions of alternative Black religious movements and its followers.

Carter's interpretation of the "Blackness" of Black religion spotlights "its relatedness to racial hierarchy as part of the knowledge and management systems of a capitalist world...[as well as] to that alternate cosmology of matter's *material multiplicity*, a cosmology of the crossroads" (Carter 2023: 11, italics added). In a word, Black religion, and more specifically the NBRMs considered in this Element, can be read as unique epistemic, cultural, and theological refusals. These religious movements functioned in the hands and sacred imaginaries of Black communities to contest and critique the status quo – the normalized conceptualizations of established religious traditions and religious authority proper – and instilled in followers a sense of hope and restored vision(s) that created new worlds of meaning. Regarding the interpretation of *blackness* in Black religion, however, I am drawn to the implications of Carter's citation of "material multiplicity," and what this might suggest for a more robust deepening of our understanding of *Black* religious movements.

Whether from the vantage point of the NOI and MSTA's pursuit of authentic Black self-knowledge, or conjurers and Spiritualists accessing supernatural resources to navigate the realities of the color line before and after Emancipation, or Father Divine's charge to create a raceless utopia in American society and beyond, each of these movements endeavored to make an intervention both against and in the midst of, a social habitus in which the matter, meaning, and making of Black humanity was disrupted by racist ontologies and social structures that limited African Americans' religious agency and religious authority. An obvious feature of reading Blackness anew, naturally takes us to the question of Black embodiment. That is, what does the study of Black religious movements reveal about the nature of Black bodies and Black ownership of the body?

Black bodies represent "problem bodies" within the context of modern race relations. In denoting the "problem" with Black bodies, on one level, I am echoing what W. E. B. Du Bois once said regarding the great chasm of the twentieth century being tied to the color line and as expressed in his central query: "What does it mean to *be* [italics mine] a problem?" To accent this point, to be a problem body effectively speaks to that body's relegation to social and essentialist ostracizing. To *be* a problem is to be lodged permanently within the realm of Otherness, which psychiatrist and philosopher Frantz Fanon once described in terms of being reduced to epidermalization – being overdetermined by external forces that assign an insidious and restrictive character to non-white racial and ethnic heritage (Fanon 2008). Charles Long also spoke to this dynamic in *Significations: Signs, Symbols, and Images in the Interpretation of Religion*. Reflecting the clash of cultures and facing the unknown, the read and reception of Black bodies amid White colonial conquest, was grounded in an "empirical otherness," which became the primary psychological point of departure prevalent in European/Western consciousness. In this social arrangement, the "extraordinariness and uniqueness of a person or culture is first recognized negatively," and made the basis upon which colonial contact, control, and coercion was justified and reified in the modern world based on the description and diagnoses for regarding the other in the relationship (Long 1986: 90).

For Black people, this overdetermination, the singular defining of Black bodies as the Other, as both problematic and always already deficient, provided opportunities to repurpose and reimagine their bodies from an insurgent vantage point. Religious agency linked to one's attire was one avenue toward this end. Examples of this included the many manifestations of bodily adornment and presentation (Neal 2025). Upon casual glance, wearing a suit and tie, or donning head coverings or turbans, is indicative of mere sartorial choice. But for the members of Black religious movements who adopted these and other bodily affectations, such interventions offered strategic practices of creative agency that (re)presented Black flesh in new, more substantive registers of meaning. The agential, insurgent, and counter-positionality afforded by new forms of self-fashioning and presentation not only revealed their spiritual and sacred significance but also countered the reductive and inferiorizing capacities of anti-Black racism. This observation is therefore in keeping with Carter's concerns about the shape of Black matter and Black religion. It was through the alternate religio-racial frameworks of these new religious movements that the matter and materiality of Black existence was given new form and therefore gifted a fluidity of shape, space, and meaning that defied the limitations of the modern racial world. Serious study and consideration of new Black religious movements likewise prompts serious acknowledgment of the host of ways in which bodily agency and the modification of the body became prominent sites through which Black communities contested the rigidities and flattening effects of race stemming from the collective White racial gaze, while also charting new ground for their own understanding of humanity and community.

Alongside embodied considerations, new religious movements underscore much of what has already been asserted regarding Black religious agency and religious authority. Notably, contending with the history of these movements reveals both an extra-church demand for spiritual sustenance and religiosity not always legible in Afro-Protestantism, as well as the capaciousness of African Americans to draw upon both spiritual and pragmatic appeal of their chosen religious enclaves in the navigation of daily life. In a word, these traditions provided tangible benefits for their followers, illustrating that the rationale(s) for their conversions likely intertwined with the hope of real, desired outcomes in the betterment of their material existence. Expressed another way, new religious movements within Black communities extend beyond the categories of protest and accommodation so often tied to African American religious orientations. Simplistic, binary frames such as these do not effectively capture the nuances, namely the motivations for why these movements take root among enthusiastic audiences, or why they engender a staying power in the larger religious marketplace.

Finally, new Black religious movements invite us to sit with the unique matter and meaning of Black lives – the nitty-gritty enfleshed life-worlds of a community engaging the ageless existential human quest for meaning. For the interpreter of religion, sitting with the histories, the beliefs, the feelings, and the thinking of Black religious movements, may pique our desire to understand, fully, their shared desires for fulfillment, self-possession, and self-transcendence. In taking up a more robust interpretation of the shape and contours of new religious movements, we are in effect opening our mind's eye to the lives and social worlds that the followers of these movements inhabit. Individual NBRMs may properly be considered case studies in historical survivalism built upon alternate faith orientations as the point of departure. These are creative disruptions that accentuate and refine the trajectories of Black humanity against the backdrop(s) of White racial empire, which is pervasive in its generative grasp in both institutional and intellectual realms, shaping both praxis and political power, as well as contemporary academia. If it is true that the story of new religio-racial movements illuminates how Black people entered into the work of racial construction in early twentieth-century America, it is necessary to see the study of religion and Black religious studies in particular as part of a methodological approach that strengthens our understanding of the many ways racialized groups navigate and negotiate the terms of their collective existence under varied regimes of power.

References

Baer, H. A. "Toward a Systematic Typology of Black Folk Healers." *Phylon* 43, no. 4 (1982): 327–43.

Baer, H. A. and M. Singer. *African American Religion: Varieties of Protest and Accommodation*, 2nd ed. Knoxville: University of Tennessee Press, 2002; first ed. 1992.

Baldwin, J. *James Baldwin: Collected Essays*. New York: Library of America, 1998.

Bowler, K. *Blessed: A History of the American Prosperity Gospel*. New York: Oxford University Press, 2013.

Braude, A. *Radical Spirits: Spiritualism and Women's Rights in Nineteenth Century America*. Bloomington: Indiana University Press, 2001; first ed. 1989.

Carter, J. K. *The Anarchy of Black Religion: A Mystic Song*. Durham, NC: Duke University Press, 2023.

CERCL Writing Collective. *Embodiment and Black Religion: Rethinking the Body in African American Religious Experience*. Sheffield: Equinox Publishing, 2017.

Chireau, Y. "Prophetess of the Spirits: Mother Leaf Anderson and the Spiritual Churches of New Orleans." In *Women Preachers and Prophets through Two Millennia of Christianity*, ed. B. M. Kienzle & P. J. Walker, 303–17. Berkeley: University of California Press, 1998.

Chireau, Y. *Black Magic: Religion and the African American Conjuring Tradition*. Berkeley: University of California Press, 2006.

Clark, E. "Noble Drew Ali's Clean and Pure Nation: The Moorish Science Temple, Identity, and Healing." *Nova Religio: The Journal of Alternative and Emergent Religions* 16, no. 3 (2013): 31–51.

Clark, E. *A Luminous Brotherhood: Afro-Creole Spiritualism in Nineteenth-Century New Orleans*. Chapel Hill: University of North Carolina Press, 2016.

Clark, E. and B. Stoddard. *Race and New Religious Movements in the United States: A Documentary Reader*. New York: Bloomsbury Academic, 2019.

Clark, K. B. and M. P. Clark. "Racial Identification and Preference among Negro Children." In *Readings in Social Psychology*, ed. E. L. Hartley. New York: Holt, Rinehart and Winston, 1947.

Cleaver, E. *Soul on Ice*. New York: Dell Publishing Company, 1968.

Curtis, E. E. IV *Islam in Black America: Identity, Liberation, and Difference in African American Islamic Thought*. Albany, NY: SUNY Press, 2002.

Dew, S. *The Aliites: Race and Law in the Religions of Noble Drew Ali*. Chicago: University of Chicago Press, 2019.

Du Bois, W. E. B. *The Souls of Black Folk*. New York: G&D Media, 2019.

Fanon, F. *Black Skin, White Masks*. New York: Grove Press, 2008.

Fauset, A. *Black Gods of the Metropolis: Negro Religious Cults of the Urban North*. Philadelphia: University of Pennsylvania Press, 2002; first edition 1944.

Finley, S. *In and Out of this World: Material and Extraterrestrial Bodies in the Nation of Islam*. Durham, NC: Duke University Press, 2022.

Glaude, E. S. Jr. *An Uncommon Faith: A Pragmatic Approach to the Study of African American Religion*. Athens: University of Georgia Press, 2018.

Greene-Hayes, A. *Underworld Work: Black Atlantic Religion Making in Jim Crow New Orleans*. Chicago: University of Chicago Press, 2025.

Griffith, R. M. "Body Salvation: New Thought, Father Divine, and the Feast of Material Pleasures." *Religion and American Culture: A Journal of Interpretation* 11, no. 2 (2001): 119–53.

Hartman, S. *Scenes of Subjection: Terror, Slavery, and Self-Making in Nineteenth Century America*. New York: Oxford University Press, 1997.

Hartman, S. *Wayward Lives, Beautiful Experiments: Intimate Histories of Riotous Black Girls, Troublesome Women, and Queer Radicals*. New York: W. W. Norton & Company, 2019.

Hopkins, D. "Slave Theology in the Invisible Institution." In *African American Religious Thought: An Anthology*, ed. C. West & E. S. Glaude, 790–830. Louisville, KY: Westminster John Knox Press, 2003.

Johnson, S. A. "The Rise of Black Ethnics: The Ethnic Turn in African American Religions, 1916–1945." *Religion and American Culture: A Journal of Interpretation* 20, no. 2 (2010): 125–63.

Johnson, S. A. *African American Religions, 1500–2000: Colonialism, Democracy, and Freedom*. New York: Cambridge University Press, 2015.

Lause, M. A. *Free Spirits: Spiritualism, Republicanism, and Radicalism in the Civil War Era*. Urbana: University of Illinois Press, 2016.

Long, C. M. *Significations: Signs, Symbols, and Images in the Interpretation of Religion*. Aurora, CO: The Davies Group, 1986.

References

Long, C. M. *Spiritual Merchants: Religion, Magic, and Commerce*. Knoxville: The University of Tennessee Press, 2001.

Lorde, A. *Sister Outsider: Essay and Speeches*. Berkeley, CA: Crossing Press, 2007.

Malcolm X. *The Autobiography of Malcolm X*. New York: Ballantine Books, 1992.

McKinnis, L. *The Black Coptic Church: Race and Imagination in a New Religion*. New York: NYU Press, 2023.

Miller, M. *Slaves to Fashion: Black Dandyism and the Styling of Black Diasporic Identity*. Durham, NC: Duke University Press, 2009.

Muhammad, E. *Message to the Blackman in America*. Chicago: The Final Call, Inc., 2012.

Muhammad, E. *How To Eat To Live*. St. John's, ANU: Brawtley Press, 2018.

Neal, L. S. *Wearing Their Faith: New Religious Movements, Dress, and Fashion in America*. Cambridge: Cambridge University Press, 2025.

Paris, P. *The Spirituality of African Peoples: The Search for a Common Moral Discourse*. Minneapolis: Fortress Press, 1994.

Patterson, O. "Authority, Alienation, and Social Death." In *African American Religious Thought: An Anthology*, ed. C. West & E. S. Glaude Jr., 99–155. Louisville, KY: Westminster John Knox Press, 2003.

Pinn, A. B. *Introducing African American Religion*. New York: Routledge, 2013.

Raboteau, A. *Slave Religion: The "Invisible Institution" in the Antebellum South*. New York: Oxford University Press, 2004 rep.; first ed. 1978.

Smith, T. *Conjuring Culture: Biblical Foundations of Black America*. New York: Oxford University Press, 1994.

Stewart, D. and T. Hucks. "Africana Religious Studies: Toward a Transdisciplinary Agenda in an Emerging Field." *Journal of Africana Religions* 1, no. 1 (2013): 28–77.

Watts, J. *God, Harlem U.S.A.: The Father Divine Story*. Berkeley: University of California Press, 1992.

Weisenfeld, J. *New World A-Coming: Black Religion and Racial Identity during the Great Migration*. New York: NYU Press, 2017.

Acknowledgments

To my parents, Rev. Dr. Derrick and Sharron Hills: Thank you for keeping me grounded.

To Jennifer Naus – it was always You. Just You. You're still the one I want to run to with all my words – all my ideas. My everything. Thank you for continuing to love me softly.

Cambridge Elements

New Religious Movements

Founding Editor

†James R. Lewis
Wuhan University

The late James R. Lewis was a Professor of Philosophy at Wuhan University, China. He was the author or co-author of 128 articles and reference book entries, and editor or co-editor of 50 books. Most recently he was the general editor for the *Alternative Spirituality and Religion Review* and served as the associate editor for the *Journal of Religion and Violence*. His prolific publications include *The Cambridge Companion to Religion and Terrorism* (Cambridge University Press 2017) and *Falun Gong: Spiritual Warfare and Martyrdom* (Cambridge University Press 2018).

Series Editor

Rebecca Moore
San Diego State University

Rebecca Moore is Emerita Professor of Religious Studies at San Diego State University. She has written and edited numerous books and articles on Peoples Temple and the Jonestown tragedy. Publications include *Beyond Brainwashing: Perspectives on Cultic Violence* (Cambridge University Press 2018) and *Peoples Temple and Jonestown in the Twenty-First Century* (Cambridge University Press 2022). She is reviews editor for *Nova Religio*, the quarterly journal on new and emergent religions published by the University of Pennsylvania Press.

About the Series

Elements in New Religious Movements go beyond cult stereotypes and popular prejudices to present new religions and their adherents in a scholarly and engaging manner. Case studies of individual groups, such as Transcendental Meditation and Scientology, provide in-depth consideration of some of the most well known, and controversial, groups. Thematic examinations of women, children, science, technology, and other topics focus on specific issues unique to these groups. Historical analyses locate new religions in specific religious social, political, and cultural contexts. These examinations demonstrate why some groups exist in tension with the wider society and why others live peaceably in the mainstream. The series highlights the differences, as well as the similarities within this great variety of religious expressions.

Cambridge Elements

New Religious Movements

Elements in the Series

Mormonism
Matthew Bowman

Jehovah's Witnesses
Jolene Chu and Ollimatti Peltonen

Wearing Their Faith: New Religious Movements, Dress, and Fashion in America
Lynn S. Neal

Santa Muerte Devotion: Vulnerability, Protection, Intimacy
Wil G. Pansters

J. Krishnamurti: Self-Inquiry, Awakening, and Transformation
Constance A Jones

Making Places Sacred: New Articulations of Place and Power
Matt Tomlinson and Yujie Zhu

Korean New Religions
Don Baker

The Revelation Spiritual Home: The Revival of African Indigenous Spirituality
Massimo Introvigne and Rosita Šorytė

Abuse in New Religious Movements
Sarah Harvey

Minority Religions, the Law, and the Courts: Cases and Consequences
James T. Richardson

New Religious Movements and the Romantic Spirit of Modernity
Stef Aupers, Dick Houtman and Galen Watts

Early Twentieth Century New Black Religious Movements in the United States
Darrius D. Hills

A full series listing is available at: www.cambridge.org/ENRM

For EU product safety concerns, contact us at Calle de José Abascal, 56–1°,
28003 Madrid, Spain or eugpsr@cambridge.org.

www.ingramcontent.com/pod-product-compliance
Lightning Source LLC
LaVergne TN
LVHW011857060526
838200LV00054B/4380